MICHELANGELO
PUBLIC AND PRIVATE

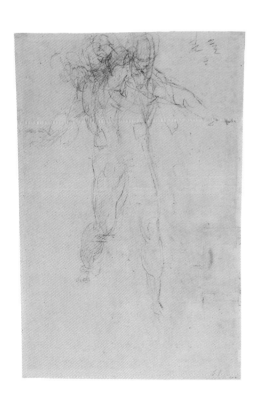

Michelangelo

PUBLIC AND PRIVATE

*Drawings for the Sistine Chapel and Other Treasures
from the Casa Buonarroti*

PINA RAGIONIERI, CURATOR

GARY M. RADKE, CURATORIAL ADVISOR

Seattle Art Museum

This book is published in conjunction with the exhibition *Michelangelo Public and Private: Drawings for the Sistine Chapel and Other Treasures from the Casa Buonarroti,* organized by the Seattle Art Museum in collaboration with the Casa Buonarroti, Florence, and on view at the Seattle Art Museum Downtown from October 15, 2009, through January 31, 2010.

LEAD PRESENTING FOUNDATION SPONSOR
Robert Lehman Foundation

PRESENTING CORPORATE SPONSORS

JPMorgan Chase & Co.

EXHIBITION SPONSORS
THE SEATTLE ART MUSEUM
SUPPORTERS

CULTURE
KING COUNTY LODGING TAX

Additional support provided by the Leona M. Geyer Charitable Trust, Enrique A. Tessada, and contributors to the Annual Fund

Text copyright © 2009 by the authors
Compilation copyright © 2009 by the Seattle Art Museum
All rights reserved.

Library of Congress Control Number: 2009934255
ISBN 978-0-932216-65-6

Page 1: Michelangelo, *Study for a Resurrected Christ,* verso (see p. 52)
Page 2: Michelangelo, *Study for a Resurrected Christ* (detail, cat. 9)

Catalogue entries by Pina Ragionieri, with additional entries by Elena Lombardi and Marcella Marongiu
Italian translation by Christian and Silvia Dupont

Edited by Suzanne Kotz
Sistine Chapel plans drawn by Rebecca Nickels
Designed by John Hubbard
Typeset in Eldorado by Marie Weiler
Color management by iocolor, Seattle
Produced by Marquand Books, Inc., Seattle
   www.marquand.com
Printed and bound in China by C&C Offset Printing Co., Ltd.

Contents

Director's Foreword

SINCE THE 1997 MILESTONE *Leonardo Lives: Leonardo da Vinci's Legacy of Art and Science*, the Seattle Art Museum has organized a series of focused exhibitions related to the greatest masters of Renaissance Italy. *Leonardo Lives* featured the artist's priceless *Codex Leicester*, a scientific document shown for the first time in the context of works of art by Leonardo and his close followers, as well as a host of twentieth-century works by artists influenced by Leonardo. In 2004 an altarpiece from Seattle's Saint James Cathedral by Florentine master Neri di Bicci was the centerpiece of another Renaissance art exhibition, this time spotlighting traditionalism in subject matter and technique. Three precious panels from Lorenzo Ghiberti's doors for Florence's Baptistery, exhibited at the museum in 2008, demonstrated why Michelangelo dubbed them the "Gates of Paradise." Now Michelangelo himself, arguably the greatest Renaissance master of all, makes his debut in Seattle thanks to the generosity of the Casa Buonarroti in the artist's hometown of Florence.

The Divine Michelangelo, as he was known to his contemporaries and later admirers, was the defining example of a Renaissance man. He called himself a sculptor—the most rugged and physically demanding of the artistic professions—but he also excelled in painting and architecture and was one of the finest Renaissance poets. He lived twice as long as many of his contemporaries, outlasting most of his friends and members of his own family. By actively participating with his biographers, notably Ascanio Condivi, he helped fashion his own larger-than-life legend for posterity. The Michelangelo we know today is in some sense a creation of the artist himself. The complexities of his personality and the often tortured history of his artistic commissions are addressed in *Michelangelo: Public and Private*, but what visitors may especially appreciate is the opportunity to witness his artistic process, which depended on drawings at almost every stage.

We are first and foremost grateful to the Casa Buonarroti, founded by the artist's grand-nephew in 1612 to preserve his memory in Florence and beyond. As the largest repository of Michelangelo's drawings, and possessing two key early sculptural reliefs, the Casa Buonarroti is well known to Renaissance scholars but less so to the general public. Director Pina Ragioneri and her staff have been most generous in sharing the collection as well as extensive knowledge of the artist with our visitors. Thanks to their generosity, Seattle can boast that it is the temporary home for twelve Michelangelo drawings, equal to the number found in American collections, public and private. It is hard to imagine that the opportunity to study this same group of original works for an extended period of time will happen again in this part of the world.

This project originated under the leadership of the museum's former director, Mimi Gardner Gates, and I hasten to congratulate her on this and the many other significant accomplishments of her tenure. Chiyo Ishikawa, Susan Brotman Deputy Director of Art and Curator of European Painting and Sculpture, has once again succeeded in developing a singular exhibition of remarkable quality in a relatively short period of time. She has both my admiration and my gratitude for all that she does at this institution, as well as for her clear vision of the highest caliber European art programs. Gary Radke, Dean's Professor of the Humanities at Syracuse University, has brought his fluency with the subject to create an engaging installation that humanizes the great artist even as we marvel at his ambition and inventiveness. Maryann Jordan, Vice-Director of the museum, enthusiastically supported the project from its earliest stages and brought her strategic thinking to many aspects of the exhibition. Michael McCafferty, Director of Exhibition Design and Museum Services, has once again created a beautiful and evocative installation. Sandra Jackson-Dumont, Kayla Skinner Director of Education, oversaw educational programs, including the production of an informative and engaging audioguide. Working under a very tight deadline, Zora Foy, Senior Manager for Exhibitions and Publications, brought her usual calm authority to the myriad details of producing the exhibition and catalogue. We are grateful to Marquand Books for the beautiful publication, and we particularly acknowledge the outstanding contributions of designer John Hubbard, as well as editor Suzanne Kotz. Finally, it is no exaggeration to say that the project could not have happened without our talented volunteers Mireya Lewin and Victoria Wilmes.

We could not have undertaken the exhibition without the early endorsement of the Robert Lehman Foundation, which has once again honored us with timely support of a special program. Our thanks, in particular, go to Philip Isles, President of the Lehman Foundation, who supported this project with extraordinary enthusiasm and immediate appreciation of its significance. We are also most grateful to our Corporate Sponsors, JPMorgan Chase and The Boeing Company, and our Exhibition Sponsors, the Seattle Art Museum Supporters (SAMS) and 4Culture King County Lodging Tax. Additional support was provided by the Leona M. Geyer Charitable Trust, Enrique A. Tessada, and contributors to the Annual Fund. The trustees of the Seattle Art Museum have my appreciation for their engagement and strong commitment to excellence.

Important projects such as *Michelangelo: Public and Private* represent the very best things that artists have created. At the same time, such endeavors reflect the large ambitions of this institution. In bringing this memorable group of original works to the Pacific Northwest, the Seattle Art Museum aims to inspire and enliven the overall cultural atmosphere of the region. Just as Michelangelo has epitomized the versatility and reputation of Renaissance artists for centuries of art lovers, we expect the Seattle Art Museum to proudly serve the breadth and depth of creative ambitions of audiences in this worthy, dynamic community.

Derrick R. Cartwright
The Illsley Ball Nordstrom Director

FIG. I. Michelangelo, *Madonna of the Steps*, c. 1490, marble. Casa Buonarroti, inv. 190.

Michelangelo Buonarroti

LIFE AND WORKS

Pina Ragionieri

MICHELANGELO WAS BORN IN CAPRESE, in the province of Arezzo, on March 6, 1475, to the Florentine Ludovico Buonarroti, at the time mayor (*podestà*) of Chiusi and Caprese, and Francesca di Neri di Miniato del Serra. At the end of his term, Ludovico returned to Florence with his family, and Michelangelo was entrusted to a wet nurse in Settignano whose family were stonemasons. According to Michelangelo's biographer Ascanio Condivi, who wrote under the guidance of the artist himself, it was this fact, together with his birth under the favor of Mercury and Venus, that caused his precocious inclination to the art of sculpture.

Michelangelo, who for his whole life defined himself as a "sculptor," began his apprenticeship in the Florentine workshop of the painters Domenico and Davide Ghirlandaio in 1487. He was introduced by his friend Francesco Granacci, against the will of his father, who had pledged him to instruction by the grammar master Francesco da Urbino. Michelangelo's frequenting of the Ghirlandaio workshop lasted only briefly, however. In fact, he was accepted in the Garden of San Marco, where Lorenzo the Magnificent de' Medici was assembling a collection of antiquities and admitting young artists so that they might be formed by the example of classical art under the direction of the sculptor Bertoldo di Giovanni. Alongside the passionate study of antiquity, Michelangelo meditated profoundly on the artists of his city's recent and glorious past. Indeed, his drawings bear witness to his interests in Giotto, Donatello, and Masaccio, in whose works, more than in those of artists from the second half of the century, he found confirmation of his aesthetic ideal of robust and essential monumentality.

Belonging to the period he spent in the home of Lorenzo the Magnificent (between 1490 and 1492) are two reliefs in marble that today are in the Casa Buonarroti—the *Madonna of the Steps* (fig. 1) and the *Battle of the Centaurs* (see fig. 3, p. 24), the earliest works that can be securely attributed to Michelangelo. In them, he already displayed the stature of a mature artist. In the first, there is an explicit reference to Donatello; in the second, to classical sculpture. But their comparison, instead of leading to the conclusion

9

that they were directly derived from these models, shows a deep assimilation and movement beyond them.

Upon the death of Lorenzo, Michelangelo left the Medici Palace to return to his family home, where he sculpted a *Hercules* in marble that was subsequently placed in the Strozzi Palace. In 1529, during the siege of Florence, Giovan Battista della Palla sold it to Francis I, king of France, who installed it at Fontainebleau in the Jardin de l'Etang. Michelangelo also executed a *Crucifix* in wood for the prior of the Convent of Santo Spirito in Florence, which Margrit Lisner, along with many critics, has recognized as the work held at Casa Buonarroti for more than thirty years before being returned to its original location in December 2000.

The years following the death of Lorenzo the Magnificent were very turbulent for the city of Florence, which was then governed by Piero de' Medici and inflamed by the preaching of the Dominican friar Girolamo Savonarola. In October 1494 Michelangelo left Florence to take refuge for a short time in Venice and then in Bologna, where he was a guest of Gian Francesco Aldrovandi. Thanks to Aldrovandi, he obtained a commission for three statues to supplement the Arca di San Domenico, which was begun in the times of Nicola Pisano (13th cent.) but remained incomplete at the death of Niccolò dell'Arca in 1494. The *Angel Holding a Candlestick*, which Michelangelo carved to match the one executed by Niccolò, is characterized by a robust physicality and intimate dynamism. It is a reminder of the influence of Jacopo della Quercia, whose relief sculptures around the portal of San Petronio in Bologna comprise one of the greatest examples of his art. Michelangelo also executed the statues *Saint Proculus* and *Saint Petronius*, in which one can sense him updating the painters of Ferrara as well as Jacopo della Quercia.

After about a year, Michelangelo went back to Florence, where he was received by Lorenzo di Pierfrancesco de' Medici, a cousin of the exiled Piero but with republican ideals, who commissioned a *Young Saint John*, sculpted in marble and since lost. Also thanks to Lorenzo, Michelangelo succeeded in selling his *Sleeping Cupid* as an antique on the Roman market. The purchaser, Cardinal Raffaele Riario, discovered the trick and demanded his money back, but he also recognized the talent of the young sculptor. He called Michelangelo to Rome and commissioned a *Bacchus* from him for the Cancelleria Palace (Museo Nazionale del Bargello, Florence). During this first Roman sojourn, he lived and worked in the home of the banker Jacopo Galli, for whom he executed another statue inspired by antiquity, which sources record as either a Cupid or an Apollo. Galli also soon came into possession of the *Bacchus*, which probably never found its way to the Cancelleria, and favored his guest with important commissions. Indeed, three contracts name Jacopo Galli as guarantor.

On August 27, 1498, Michelangelo signed his first contract for a public work, a *Pietà* in marble (fig. 2), requested by Cardinal Jean Bilhères de Lagraulas, ambassador of Charles VIII to the papal court, for the chapel of the Madonna della Febbre. The *Pietà*, today in Saint Peter's Basilica in the Vatican, is the only work signed by Buonarroti. It represents one of his highest achievements, not only for the virtuosity with which he rendered the tactile sense of the surfaces and the anatomical perfection, but also for the psychological intensity of the grouping, in which the tragic event is sublimated in a tranquil meditation on the mystery of the Incarnation and Redemption.

Jacopo Galli also surely played an important role in the commission of an altarpiece for the church of Sant'Agostino, most likely the *Entombment of Christ* now in the National Gallery, London. It remained unfinished in the spring of 1501 when Michelangelo left Rome for Florence. The *Entombment*, nevertheless, is not the only painting Buonarroti executed during his Roman sojourn. Vasari mentions the *Stigmatization of Saint Francis*, for which Michelangelo would have supplied the cartoon to a painter, recently identified as Piero d'Argenta, a collaborator of Buonarroti from Ferrara. According to Hirst (1994), the panel *Madonna with the Christ Child, Saint John, and Angels*, known as the Manchester Madonna (National Gallery, London), referred to in a payment of June 1497, was also begun in Rome.

Michelangelo left Rome in March 1501, having been summoned to Florence, according to Vasari, "by several of his friends . . . because it was not out of the question that from that ruined marble block that was in the Opera [del Duomo] he might carve a figure, as he had already wanted to do." It is nevertheless not clear whether he returned to Florence for the commission of the statue *David*, to which Vasari refers, or for an earlier one, for which he would have already made the agreements in Rome, as the presence of Jacopo Galli as guarantor seems to confirm. In fact, the contract that Michelangelo signed with Cardinal Francesco Todeschini Piccolomini, the future Pope Pius III, was dated June 5, 1501. According to it, Michelangelo was to execute in the place of Pietro Torrigiano—a Florentine sculptor who was a contemporary of Michelangelo and who, like him, was educated in the Garden of San Marco—fifteen statues for the completion of the Piccolomini Altar (1483–85) in the cathedral of Siena, created by Andrea Bregno.

Of the fifteen statues that were envisioned, only four were executed (*Saint Peter, Saint Paul, Saint Pius,* and *Saint Gregory*), because over the next four years Michelangelo was busy in Florence with much more important public and private commissions. He worked on the block of marble at the Opera del Duomo from which he carved *David* (fig. 3), finished in 1503 and placed in the Piazza della Signoria in 1504 as a symbol of civic virtues (today it stands in the Galleria dell'Accademia in Florence). In August 1502 the magistrate (*gonfaloniere*) Piero Soderini and the city's eight priors charged him to execute a *David* in bronze for Pierre de Rohan, an influential member of the French court. In April of the following year, Michelangelo agreed to create statues in marble of the twelve apostles to be placed in the interior of the Duomo in Florence, of which only the unfinished *Saint Matthew* (Galleria dell'Accademia, Florence) remains. In December 1503 payments began for another work in marble, a *Madonna and Child* commissioned by the Flemish merchant Alexandre Mouscron and destined for his chapel in the cathedral of Bruges. Yet the most important commission

FIG. 2. Michelangelo, *Pietà*, 1498–99, marble. Saint Peter's Basilica, Vatican City.

FIG. 3. Michelangelo, *David*, 1503, marble. Galleria dell'Accademia, Florence.

FIG. 4. Michelangelo, *Holy Family with the Infant Saint John the Baptist (Doni Tondo)*, 1503–4, tempera on panel. Galleria degli Uffizi, Florence.

came to him in the summer of 1504, when Soderini proposed that Michelangelo fresco an episode from the Battle of Cascina on a wall of the Sala Grande del Consiglio in the Palazzo Vecchio, where Leonardo was already painting his *Battle of Anghiari*. This grandiose project, which permitted Michelangelo to measure himself against the art of the older master, remained unfinished on account of his departure from Florence. He executed only preparatory designs and the cartoon, which all of Buonarroti's contemporaries and younger artists studied and which Vasari called "more a divine than human creation." The remains of the cartoon were preserved during the 1500s in Mantua by the Strozzis and during the 1600s in Torino in the Sabaudian collections.

Michelangelo dedicated equal effort and innovation to several important private commissions that date to these years. They consist of the marble tondos *Madonna and Child with the Young Saint John the Baptist*, sculpted for the wealthy patrons Taddeo Taddei (Royal Academy of Fine Arts, London) and Bartolomeo Pitti (Museo Nazionale del Bargello, Florence), and the painting *Holy Family with the Infant Saint John the Baptist* (fig. 4), which he completed for the merchant Agnolo Doni.

In March 1505 Michelangelo returned to Rome, having been called by Pope Julius II to create the pope's mausoleum for the Vatican basilica. Michelangelo intended it to be a grandiose work, one that would exceed in size and beauty every other ancient and modern monument. Michelangelo proposed an independent structure, rectangular in form, consisting of three levels decorated with marble statues and bronze reliefs. Once the project was approved, Michelangelo went to Carrara to look for marble, but upon his return to Rome, the pope had already changed his mind and abandoned the ambitious plan. Deeply hurt by this behavior,

Michelangelo left the city, with papal emissaries pursuing him to no avail. Thus began what Condivi, surely borrowing the words of the artist, called the "tragedy of the tomb," a torment that lasted forty years.

A reconciliation between the two took place in Bologna at the end of 1506 and was sealed by the commission of a bronze portrait of the pope, to be installed in a niche on the façade of San Petronio. Having finished this work (which was destroyed just five years later, after the restoration of the Signoria of the Bentivoglio), Michelangelo returned to Rome to paint the frescoes on the ceiling of the Sistine Chapel—a charge he accepted with a certain reluctance and which he pursued in complete isolation. He experienced it as a challenge not only for the vastness and difficulty of the labor, but also for the desire to go beyond the limits imposed by tradition and the levels he himself had attained. The vaulted ceiling, frescoed with the story of humanity *ante legem*—before the Law of Moses—and with the figures of prophets and sibyls and of the forebears of Christ, was finished in 1512, after four years of intense labor. Shortly afterward Julius II died, and Michelangelo signed with his heirs a new contract for the pope's funerary monument which redefined the grandiose dimensions of the preceding version. For this project Michelangelo executed two statues, *Slaves*, now at the Louvre, and *Moses* (fig. 5), which was later recovered for the final version of the tomb in the church of San Pietro in Vincoli in Rome.

FIG. 5. Michelangelo, *Moses* (from the tomb of Pope Julius II), c. 1515, marble. San Pietro in Vincoli, Rome.

FIG. 6. Michelanagelo,
*Model for the Façade of San
Lorenzo, Florence,* c. 1518,
wood. Casa Buonarroti,
inv. 518.

The "tragedy of the tomb" was not yet destined for conclusion, because the new pope,
Leo X (Giovanni de' Medici, son of Lorenzo the Magnificent), called Buonarroti back to
Florence to charge him with designing the façade of the basilica of San Lorenzo, which had
been left unfinished by Brunelleschi. For three years Michelangelo worked on various designs, settling upon a model that revolutionized the traditional concept of a façade. Ignoring
the preexisting structure, he imagined a plastic body in which architectonic structure and
sculptural decoration constituted an indissoluble unity characterized by strong volumetric
and luminous contrasts (fig. 6).

Once again, however, the work was not completed. The pope abandoned the project for
financial reasons and proceeded with the construction of only one chapel, mirroring the Sacristy of Brunelleschi, which was destined to house the tombs of the Magnificent, his brother
Giuliano, and two dukes who had recently died. Michelangelo took the Old Sacristy as an
example, accentuating the dynamic tension of the framework and its verticality. He envisioned
twin funerary monuments, placed in the walls flanking the altar, to hold the sepulchers of
Lorenzo, duke of Urbino, and Giuliano, duke of Nemours (fig. 7). Beneath the statues of
the two "Captains," ensconced on the sarcophagi, the personifications of Time found their
places: *Dawn, Dusk, Day,* and *Night.* At the base, there were to have been river deities, for
which Michelangelo made only the models. On the end wall he put the tombs of the Magnificent and Giuliano, with statues of the Madonna and Child and the patron saints of the
Medici, Saint Cosmas and Saint Damian, which were sculpted respectively by Giovanni
Angelo Montorsoli and Raffaello da Montelupo. In 1524 Pope Clement VII (Giuliano's son)
gave Michelangelo a commission to design a library to be built in the San Lorenzo complex
to house the valuable volumes collected by his ancestors.

In spite of these weighty burdens, Michelangelo managed to dedicate himself to other
projects, such as the design of the "kneeling windows" (pedimented windows supported
by volutes) for the Medici Palace and the statue of the *Risen Christ* for the Roman church
of Santa Maria sopra Minerva. Michelangelo signed the contract with his patrons Bernardo
Cenci, Mario Scappucci, and Metello Vari in June 1514, pledging that he would deliver the
statue within four years. Nevertheless, after two years of labor, on account of a flaw in the
marble, he abandoned the work and began to sculpt a new version, which he sent to Rome

FIG. 7. Interior view of the New Sacristy of San Lorenzo with the Medici tombs, 1519–33, Florence.

in the spring of 1512, when it was all but complete. There it was given finishing touches and installed by Pietro Urbano.

In 1527, after the Sack of Rome, the Medici were chased out of Florence, and a republican regime was established. Michelangelo, having left the project at San Lorenzo, was loyal to the new government, for which he took up work again on the group, to be placed as a pendant to *David*, that had been commissioned twenty years earlier by Soderini's republic. Michelangelo quickly abandoned the group, which he had reconceived from representing Hercules and Cacus to Samson and a Philistine, because he was elected to the Committee of Nine on Military Affairs (Nove della Milizia) and charged with instituting a system of fortifications for Florence, which was already then being besieged by imperial troops. This duty also led him to Alfonso I d'Este and Ferrara, where he studied the city's defensive systems and from whom he received a commission for the painting *Leda and the Swan*, inspired by antiquity in both its subject and iconography. The work, however, never entered the Estense collections and was sold to Francis I of France by Antonio Mini, an apprentice to Michelangelo who had received it as a gift from his master.

Despairing the fate of the Florentine republic, Michelangelo left the city on September 21, 1529, to take refuge in France at the court of Francis I. The journey was interrupted, however, in Venice, and at the end of the year Michelangelo resumed his work in Florence. But the Florentine republic was counting its days, and in August of the following year the Medici returned to the city. During this time Michelangelo sculpted an *Apollo* for Baccio Valori (Bargello, Florence) and, after obtaining a pardon from Clement VII, returned to the tasks of the Sacristy and the Laurentian Library.

He also renewed contact with the heirs of Julius II, which in April 1532 resulted in a new contract (the fourth, after those of 1505, 1513, and 1516) and a new project for the tomb, no longer to be realized in the Vatican basilica but in San Pietro in Vincoli. The monument, which by now had lost its freestanding structure in favor of a wall tomb configuration, was to include eleven statues, six by Michelangelo and five by other artists, not counting the four *Slaves* (Galleria dell'Accademia, Florence), which remained unfinished, and *Victory* (Palazzo Vecchio, Florence). The artist simultaneously supervised workshops in Rome and Florence, dividing his time between them in the years 1532–34. Also dating to this time is the elaboration

FIG. 8. Aerial view of Piazza del Campidoglio, Rome.

of the cartoons of religious and mythological subjects whose painted realization the artist entrusted to Sebastiano del Piombo or Jacopo da Pontormo.

It was perhaps for Clement VII's massive project for the altar wall of the Sistine Chapel, a fresco of the *Last Judgment* (see fig. 14, p. 82), or perhaps for the friendship that bound the artist to the young Tommaso dei Cavalieri, whom he met in 1532, that in September 1534 Michelangelo moved permanently to Rome. There he attended to the work for the tomb of Julius II and the *Last Judgment*, leaving the New Sacristy to be completed by other artists according to the models he provided. To complete the *Last Judgment*, Michelangelo returned to the Sistine Chapel after almost forty years. During this time his art had lost the classical harmony that characterized his paintings for the ceiling, becoming, in this fresco, an apocalyptic vision in which no harmonious or rational laws exist, but where instead the whole surface, deprived of depth, is animated by the swirling movement of figures with robust bodies and contorted faces.

Clement VII was succeeded by the Farnese pope Paul III, who confirmed Michelangelo's commission for the *Last Judgment* while freeing him from any obligation to the heirs of Julius II. The pope then named him "chief architect, sculptor, and painter of the Apostolic Palaces" and entrusted him with the urban planning of the square on the Capitoline Hill (fig. 8). In the center of the piazza, Michelangelo placed the Roman equestrian statue of *Marcus Aurelius* and then designed the monumental stairway, senatorial palace, and conservators' palace, whose installation Tommaso dei Cavalieri supervised as a deputy to the Capitoline construction. Upon the death of Antonio da Sangallo il Giovane (1546), Michelangelo became responsible for the completion of the Farnese Palace. His intervention

FIG. 9. Dome of Saint Peter's Basilica, Rome.

in the façade and courtyard, while respecting what was already there, gave the building a plastic dynamism. He was also named architect for the construction of Saint Peter's, for which he abandoned Sangallo's plan, which had combined the model of a central layout with a longitudinal one, and returned to Bramante's idea of a central layout with a Greek cross inscribed in a square. He designed the apses and the dome (fig. 9), and conferred unity upon the exterior through a gigantic order of Corinthian pilasters, upon which rests an attic running around the entire building.

During the pontificate of Paul III the "tragedy of the tomb" finally ended. Thanks to the intervention of the pope, a new contract was signed (August 20, 1542) that called for the completion of the monument to Julius II with the statues that Michelangelo had already finished (*Moses* and the Louvre *Slaves*, later substituted by the statues of *Rachel* and *Leah*) along with three others (*Madonna and Child*, *Prophet*, and *Sibyl*) sculpted under his direction by Raffaello da Montelupo. While he was painting the fresco of the *Last Judgment*, Michelangelo created the marble bust *Brutus* for the Florentine exile Niccolò Ridolfi, who in his pride incarnated the republican ideals of the artist and his position with respect to the Florentine political situation.

With the Sistine frescoes unveiled in 1541 and the final contract signed with Julius's heirs, Paul III asked Michelangelo to create frescoes of the *Conversion of Saint Paul* (fig. 10) and the *Crucifixion of Saint Peter* for the Pauline Chapel in the Vatican. Even more than the *Last Judgment*, these frescoes demonstrate the profound rift in the artist's conscience, which was disturbed by the events that had overwhelmed the Church in those years. Contributing to Buonarroti's movement toward a reformist position was the Roman poetess Vittoria Colonna, with whom Michelangelo held a deep friendship and for whom he created a few works with religious subjects.

The artist's decision to sculpt a *Pietà* for his own tomb should also be seen in this same perspective. During the latter part of his life, in fact, Michelangelo applied himself less and less to painting and sculpture in order to concentrate on his architectural studies. His last two sculptures are two versions of the *Pietà:* the first (Museo dell'Opera del Duomo, Florence, fig. 11), already begun in 1550, was almost finished when Michelangelo noticed a crack that induced him to mutilate and abandon the block. The sculpture was sold to Francesco Badini, who had it finished by Tibero Calcagni, a student of Buonarroti. He began a second version (Castello Sforzesco, Milan, fig. 12), on which he would work until his death, though he was never satisfied with the results. Indeed, only death interrupted Michelangelo's incessant searching: he changed the position of Christ and his Mother several times, reaching a point of extreme essentialism and intense drama.

The duty of architect for the construction of Saint Peter's was confirmed by the successors to Paul III. For Buonarroti, the completion of the basilica represented a kind of expiation for sins. He asked that the contract expressly state that "he was serving the construction for the love of God without any reward," and in response to requests by Cosimo I de' Medici to return to Florence he replied that to abandon the labor would be "the cause of great ruin to the construction of Saint Peter's, a great shame, and a very great sin." Although the duke

FIG. 10. Michelangelo, *Conversion of Saint Paul*, 1542–45, fresco. Pauline Chapel, Vatican Palace, Rome.

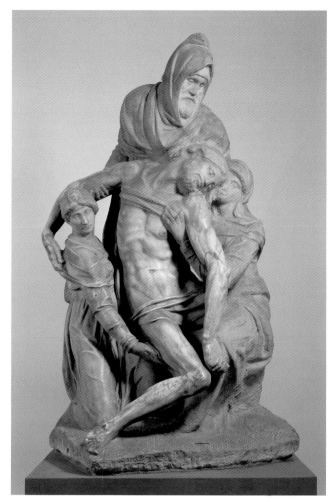

did not succeed in bringing Michelangelo back to Florence, he obtained from him a commitment to design the church of the Florentine community in Rome. Around 1559–60, Buonarroti worked up several designs featuring a central layout imposed on the form of a circle or square and animated by a strong dynamic tension. The central layout motif was also evident in the Sforza Chapel in Santa Maria Maggiore, the design of which dates to around 1560. The last years of the artist's life also witnessed the completion of designs for the Porta Pia, commissioned by Pope Paul IV as a scenographic finish to the new street that he had opened between the Quirinale and the Aurelian walls. Michelangelo's architectural activities ended with the transformation of the Baths of Diocletian into the church of Santa Maria degli Angeli.

On February 18, 1564, at nearly ninety years of age, Michelangelo died in his house in Rome, the Macel de' Corvi, in the company of his dearest friends, among them Tommaso dei Cavalieri and Daniele da Volterra. Just one month earlier, the congregation of the Council of Trent had decreed that the parts of the *Last Judgment* regarded as obscene be covered over, a gesture that showed the most complete misunderstanding not only of Michelangelo's art but of his intense spirituality.

FIG. 11. Michelangelo, *Pietà*, c. 1457–55, marble. Museo dell'Opera del Duomo, Florence.

FIG. 12. Michelangelo, *Rondanini Pietà*, 1552–64, marble. Castello Sforzesco, Milan.

FIG. 1. Giuliano Finelli (1601 or 1602–1653), *Bust of Michelangelo Buonarroti the Younger,*
1630, marble. Casa Buonarroti, inv. 294.

Casa Buonarroti

NOT JUST A MUSEUM

Pina Ragionieri

Via Ghibellina is a historic street in the center of Florence lined with
ancient houses and palaces. Walking down it, one comes upon a noble seventeenth-century
building at number 70 whose very name, Casa Buonarroti, evokes a significant past. Its most
well-known aspect is naturally the museum, which contains several masterpieces by Michelangelo, including the two icons of the Casa: the marble reliefs of the *Madonna of the Steps*
and the *Battle of the Centaurs*, executed in Florence by the artist when he was just an adoles-
cent. They are penetrating witnesses: first to his deep study of Donatello and second to his
unquenched passion for classical art. The museum also holds rich collections of paintings,
sculptures, ceramics, and archaeological fragments brought together in various ways by the
Buonarroti family over several generations. In addition, the Casa houses the largest collection in the world of autograph drawings by Michelangelo and the invaluable papers of the
Buonarroti family's centuries-old archives.

A deed of sale, a document already known to Gaetano Milanesi in 1875 and published
in 1965 by Ugo Procacci, shows that on March 3, 1508, Michelangelo bought, for the price
of 1,050 large florins, three houses and a cottage located between the Via Ghibellina and the
present Via Michelangelo Buonarroti. The artist purchased another small adjoining house
in April 1514. Of these five houses, three were most likely rented out at once, while it is certain that from 1516 Michelangelo, along with his household, occupied the two most spacious
ones whenever his Medici patrons did not prompt him to look for marble blocks in Carrara
or Pietrasanta. In 1525, at the urging of Pope Clement VII, he moved to Via Mozza to be
closer to the construction of San Lorenzo, which, since 1516, had seen him engrossed in complex undertakings: the troubled project for the façade of the basilica (which, as we know,
remained unfinished), the New Sacristy, and the Laurentian Library.

From 1525, the modest compound in Via Ghibellina was entirely rented out. Michelangelo lived elsewhere. Yet in his letters a constant worry, even obsession, may be discerned
over entrusting his family's name to the building in Florence in such a way that in the future
it might distinguish them with the highest level of nobility and prestige.

For one who has worked inside Casa Buonarroti for many years now, going back to Michelangelo prompts reflections about his private life, seeing him in the modest dwelling where he lived for a few years, while still young, in Via Ghibellina. From this time there remain a few traces inside the seventeenth-century palace. He was parsimonious toward himself, but always ready, as one knows, to support his family, and especially desirous that his own should live in "an honorable house in the city."

The letters of the artist give ample, sometimes even moving, accounts of his affection for his family. To give an example from among the least known, the papers of the Buonarroti archives transport us to the middle of the sixteenth century, when Michelangelo had already for some years left Florence for Rome (this took place in 1534 and proved to be a one-way journey). By then, he had already lived past seventy years, and thoughts of death inhabited his mind with ever greater frequency. Perhaps it was for this reason that he wanted so much for his beloved nephew Leonardo (1519–1599), son of Buonarotto, Michelangelo's older brother—the only one in whom he could entrust his hope for the continuation of his lineage— to finally marry, and not only that, but to go on to live in a home that was worthy of the family. From the letters of Michelangelo, these private, humble preoccupations plainly emerge, as in these words, directed to his nephew in 1547:

> . . . when it seems to you that you should take a wife, as seems necessary to me, the house where you live will not serve the need. If you should find that you cannot buy something suitable, I think that I could enlarge where you stay in Via Ghibellina . . .

And again, two years later:

> You need someone who can stay by your side and whom you can command, someone who does not want to chase after pomp and go to weddings and feasts everyday, because where there is a court, it is easy to become a whore, especially for those without relatives. And it is not partial to say that it is fitting that you wish to ennoble yourself, because it is well known that we are ancient citizens of Florence and as noble as any other family . . .

Recounted through the letters to Leonardo, this private worried solicitation of Michelangelo was placated only by its happy ending (which, we should remember, took place while the sculptor was consumed with that heartbreaking *Pietà* he would have liked to have had upon his tomb):

February 16, 1550:
> You wrote me some time ago that you wanted to work on the house in Via Ghibellina, not finding any other house to buy; since then I don't know what you have done about it . . .

August 7, 1550:
> Regarding the matter of taking a wife, we do not talk about it anymore. I have been told by everyone that I should give you a wife, as if I had a thousand of them in the bag.

March 25, 1553:
> Leonardo, I know from your latest letter how, concerning the taking of a wife, you have made arrangements to have the Ridolfi girl. It must have been four months or more that I answered regarding the two possibilities you wrote me about, both of whom I liked, but then you did not write me anything more. I do not understand and do not know what your ideas are. This treatment has already gone on long enough to tear at me so that I no longer know what to write to you.

Regarding this Ridolfi girl, in case you do not have any good information to make you happy, I do. What I wrote to you on other occasions about the substance (that is, the dowry), I reaffirm. If you would not like to marry her, or any other, I leave the worry to you. I have waited sixty years on your situation. I am now old, and need to think of myself. Indeed, take a wife you like, because what you will do will be for yourself, and not for me, for I have only a little time left.

April 22, 1553:

From your letter, I know how the arrangements for the consideration of Donato Ridolfi's daughter have concluded. May God be thanked, praying that it should follow with his grace.

May 20, 1553:

From your last letter, I know that you have your wife at home and that you are very content, and that you pass along her greetings to me. . . . The satisfaction you have gives me great pleasure, and I thank God continually as much as a man knows how and can.

October 24, 1553:

From your letter, I know that Cassandra is pregnant, which makes me very happy because I can truly hope that we will have some kind of heir, whether feminine or masculine. God is to be thanked for everything.

April 21, 1554:

I gather from your last letter that Cassandra gave birth to a beautiful little boy, that she is well, and that he will be called Buonarroto—all of which brought me great joy. Let God be thanked, and let me do it well, so that He will bring us honor and preserve our family.

From the birth of the firstborn, fourteen years would pass before Cassandra gave birth to the son who was destined to "maintain the household"—the one who would know how to derive from the modest home of Leonardo the building in Florence to which his great ancestor had at length and in vain aspired: the Casa Buonarroti as it appears to us today. It was 1568. They gave him the name Michelangelo, in memory of his famous uncle, who by then had been dead four years.

Michelangelo Buonarroti the Younger (1568 1647) was a figure of great prominence in the cultural panorama of Florence in the first half of the seventeenth century (fig. 1). Until now, he has been studied more as a literary figure, man of the theater, and author of two famous comedies, *La Tancia* and *La Fiera*, than as an exceptionally versatile and entrepreneurial cultural organizer, and friend and generous host of artists and scientists. Still for the most part unpublished are the numerous volumes of his papers—letters relating to the administration of his household and other writings kept in the Buonarroti archives which could bring to life, if properly researched, an interesting intellectual portrait that has only been glimpsed up until now.

Michelangelo the Younger expanded the property holdings. It was through his initiative that between 1612 and 1640 the Casa assumed the physiognomy that today is rather faithfully preserved. To him we owe the creation of four monumental rooms on the *piano nobile* (the second floor) that are meant to celebrate the glory of his revered great-uncle and the greatness of the family. They feature a decorative plan that was rather complex, personally elaborated by the owner of the house, who among other things minutely recorded events, payments, and dates so that today no doubts remain about the identities of the creators of the works and

FIG. 2. The Gallery, Casa Buonarroti.

FIG. 3. Michelangelo, *Battle of the Centaurs*, 1490–92, marble. Casa Buonarroti, inv. 192.

their dates of execution. The most worthy artists working in Florence at the time were called to work on the project. In these rooms, which have remained miraculously intact through more than a few events and renovations, a visitor can still get a sampling of the highest level of seventeenth-century Florentine and Tuscan figurative art.

The first room, called the Gallery (fig. 2), crafted between 1613 and 1635, takes for its theme the praise of Michelangelo the artist, man, and poet, which unfolds through a unique biography in images. Here, in a position of honor, was placed the extraordinary marble relief that Michelangelo had sculpted when he was no older than seventeen at the school of sculptor Bertoldo di Giovanni in the Garden of San Marco: the *Battle of the Centaurs*, which still today is the emblematic work of the Casa and its museum (fig. 3). The relief remained here until 1875, under a large painting that Michelangelo the Younger had acquired thinking it was an original by his great ancestor (in reality it was a work based on a cartoon by Michelangelo executed by his student and biographer Ascanio Condivi [c. 1525–1574]).

Work on the second room, the Room of Night and Day, was begun in 1624 and continued for years. In 1625 Jacopo Vignali painted a fresco on the ceiling, *God the Father Separating Light from Darkness*, and the personifications of night and day that give the room its name. The most unique characteristic of this room is the little space embellished by delicate frescoes and closed off with shutters like a closet—the Writing Cabinet to which Michelangelo the Younger frequently withdrew (fig. 4). The frescoed decoration continues on the walls with depictions of members of the family. In addition, the room is adorned with important works of art, among which are the predella with the *Life of Saint Nicholas of Bari*, a masterpiece by Giovanni di Francesco, a painter active in Florence in the mid-fifteenth century; a portrait of Michelangelo executed by Giuliano Bugiardini; and a bronze bust of the artist by Daniele da Volterra (see cat. no. 3).

FIG. 4. The Writing Cabinet, Room of Night and Day, Casa Buonarroti.

FIG. 5. Room of the Angels,
Casa Buonarroti.

FIG. 6. The Study, Casa
Buonarroti.

The sequence continues with the Room of the Angels, used as a chapel beginning in 1677 (fig. 5). Frescoes on the walls by Jacopo Vignali represent the figures of saints who march in procession from the church militant toward the church triumphant. Here one admires, above the altar table, the large wooden intarsia based on a cartoon by Pietro da Cortona depicting the Madonna and Child, which can be dated to about 1642. In this same room is the famous marble bust by Giuliano Finelli, a student of Bernini, portraying Michelangelo the Younger (see fig. 1).

The fourth room, the Study (fig. 6), whose preparation dates to 1633–37, displays high upon the walls a picturesque series of notable and faithfully reproduced portraits of illustrious Tuscans, painted by Cecco Bravo, Matteo Rosselli, and Domenico Pugliani. Beneath the frescoes runs a series of wooden cabinets with inlays in ivory and mother of pearl, alternating with vitrines behind which are kept many of the family's collection registries.

The four rooms, followed by a smaller room where Michelangelo the Younger liked to gather together numerous items from his collection, remained intact throughout the centuries—a unique situation for the interior of the palace. For example, during a renovation in the early nineteenth century, another contribution of Michelangelo the Younger was almost completely lost: a kind of roof garden, located in the colonnade of the penthouse, that even had a grotto with stucco decorations, artificial porous rocks, and water effects.

Two of Michelangelo the Younger's essential characteristics—his passion for collecting and his veneration of his family's past—are the basis for the formation of the artistic heritage of the family. Redounding to his merit are acquisitions of ancient sculpture: it was he who wanted to place in a preeminent position in the first monumental room the *Battle of the Centaurs;* it was he who negotiated with the sacristan of Santa Croce for the acquisition of the predella with the *Life of Saint Nicholas of Bari* (fig. 7; "one of the most beautiful products of fifteenth-century Florence," according to Robert Longhi); it is to him that Casa Buonarroti owes the recovery of the *Madonna of the Steps* (see fig. 1, p. 8) and not a few original drawings of Michelangelo, which, after the death of the artist, and certainly before 1568, had been involuntarily surrendered to the Medici collections.

At this point it would be good to consider what is perhaps the most valuable treasure of the house: the collection of Michelangelo's drawings. Vasari says that Michelangelo, "shortly before he died, burned a great number of the drawings, sketches, and cartoons composed in his own hand so that no one might see the labors he endured and the ways in which he tested his genius in order not to appear anything but perfect." This great bonfire, accomplished in two episodes, was the most conspicuous but presumably not the only one. This is why the corpus of Buonarroti's drawings is so incomplete and, at times, problematic from the

FIG. 7. Giovanni di Francesco (1412–1459), *Life of Saint Nicholas of Bari* (detail), c. 1457, tempera on panel. Casa Buonarroti, inv. 68.

perspective of attribution, because it is impossible to trace in a continuous line the passages that accompanied the artistic progress of his long life.

The drastic destructions notwithstanding, there remained at the time of Michelangelo's death some drawings that were already for sale on the market, especially in Rome; many sheets left in Florence at the family home; and not a few drawings that he had given to friends. Concerning these gifts, the artist undoubtedly believed in the imperfection (that is, in the preparatory and temporary nature) of the graphic mark, and he used and reused sheets for various purposes. Yet throughout the years Michelangelo made gifts of drawings to friends who were particularly dear to him. Such are the works that today are called, according to the apt designation of Johannes Wilde, "presentation drawings." They are highly elaborated works, classically finished and concerned with complex subjects, often profane and sometimes not easy to interpret. Among the beneficiaries were Gherardo Perini, Tommaso dei Cavalieri, and Vittoria Colonna. They are drawings that survived the destructive fury of the artist not only because they were jealously guarded by their owners but also because of their being, after all, "perfect."

On the other hand, we must remember that an idea had come to Cosimo I de' Medici to collect the drawings of famous artists while Michelangelo was still alive, even though by that time he had resided for many years in Rome, far from what was happening in the Florentine court. With the aim of fulfilling his collecting desires, the duke did not turn to Buonarroti directly but instead to the aforementioned Tommaso dei Cavalieri, the young Roman patrician who had been a friend of Michelangelo since 1532 and the recipient of the largest grouping— extraordinary for its quality—of presentation drawings. Already in 1562, two years before the death of his great friend, Cavalieri found himself obliged to give to Cosimo I the splendid *Cleopatra*—which he had received as a gift from Michelangelo about thirty years earlier— although he could not keep himself from stating in the letter accompanying the forced surrender that to be deprived of the drawing caused him as much suffering as losing a child. In order to get more works, there is every indication that Cosimo I awaited the death of the great old man and an easily foreseeable "inheritance."

It is therefore no wonder that Cosimo I, in a letter sent to his ambassador Serristori less than a month after the death of Michelangelo, would label the artist's burning of drawings "an act not worthy of him," while noting the great disappointment felt in the Florentine court on account of Michelangelo's decision, which took from the duke a patrimony he already considered his own. It was thus that Vasari warmly advised Leonardo Buonarroti, Michelangelo's nephew and heir, to first of all beg the duke's pardon for the "misdeed of his uncle," and, moreover, to offer him what still remained of the artist's work in his studio in Via Mozza in Florence as a consolation gift. In a letter dated March 4, 1564, written to Serristori the day before the ducal complaint, Vasari pleaded:

> *Neither would it seem to me inopportune, my dear Messer Lionardo, . . . that your lordship should write a letter to his Excellency expressing regret for the loss that has befallen the city and his Excellency in this death, and that—as I saw you wrote—you grieve on account of [Michelangelo] not having left either drawings, or cartoons or models because you had planned to share them with him. But since he is gone and has left everything to you only, write to him that in faith and in servitude you will be the same as your uncle, and that because nothing is left except the things in Via Mozza, they will be his, if it pleases him, praying that he not fail in giving you the same protection while you are alive that he had given to Michelangelo before he passed into the next life.*

Leonardo promptly obeyed but went even further, giving to Cosimo the very beautiful marble relief of the *Madonna of the Steps*, which had always belonged to the family, and buying back at high cost on the Roman market the few yet most precious items that were still available. Among these was the splendid sheet with the *Annunciation*, still today in the prints and drawings room of the Galleria degli Uffizi. Thus, by this means, as we learn once more from Vasari, many "drawings, sketches, and cartoons in Michelangelo's hand" passed into the Medici collections. A few months later, when Gherardo Perini died, "three sheets with some 'divine heads' in black chalk" became the property of Francesco de' Medici, "prince of Florence, who keeps them as jewels, as indeed they are." Even the "divine heads," now positively identified by scholars, are likewise still present in the voluminous catalogue of the Uffizi's prints and drawings room.

When Michelangelo Buonarroti the Younger decided to prepare a series of monumental rooms in the family home in Via Ghibellina, transforming part of his own quarters into a museum dedicated to the memory of his great ancestor and to the exaltation of the family's accomplishments, the *Madonna of the Steps* and a portion of the drawings given to the Medici were restored to him, as a token of high esteem, by Grand Duke Cosimo II. Among the drawings of Michelangelo that returned home there was a new and very valuable acquisition: the famous drawing depicting Cleopatra that Cavalieri with much pain had given up to the Medici collections. For Michelangelo the Younger, the arrival in Casa Buonarroti of a work so extraordinary, and remarkable for the biographical exchanges mentioned above, was thus of great importance. It is no wonder that such a thoughtful grandnephew wanted to display it in his Writing Cabinet, the small, refined room to which he withdrew to attend to his studies.

In those years still more sheets by Michelangelo that seemed particularly beautiful to the owner of the house were framed and hung on the walls of the new rooms: for example, in the Room of Night and Day, one of the preliminary drawings for the façade of San Lorenzo, and, in the Room of the Angels, the small cartoon of the *Madonna and Child* (fig. 8)—undoubtedly one of the most moving masterpieces in the collection. Most of the drawings, however, were gathered together in volumes, which were neatly arranged in the cabinets of the Study.

From this time on, the drawings of Michelangelo that remained in the Medici collection and those that were reverently preserved by Michelangelo the Younger constituted two independent nuclei. The collection belonging to the Buonarroti family, which was enriched soon thereafter by a few items owned by Buontalenti, was the largest in the world at the time, and it remains so today, with more than two hundred sheets, despite the serious assaults it suffered. Indeed, at the end of the eighteenth century it was impoverished by an initial sale made by the revolutionary Filippo Buonarroti to the painter and collector Jean-Baptiste Wicar, and by a second sale, in October 1859, that the Cavalier Michelangelo Buonarroti made to the British Museum.

In 1858 Michelangelo's last direct heir, Cosimo Buonarroti, died. He possessed the most complete portion of Michelangelo's papers, and in his will, he left them, together with the palace in Via Ghibellina and its contents, for public enjoyment. From that time, even during difficult years for the institution, the drawings were permanently displayed in the museum in frames and display cases. Only in 1960 were they finally delivered from the "humiliating defeat" of a "careless custody" that had caused not a few damages to the sheets, as Paola Barocchi, who initiated this truly meritorious action, recounts. Giovanni Poggi, the well-respected Michelangelo scholar, was then director of the Casa Buonarroti, and Giulia Sinibaldi was the chief of the prints and drawings room at the Uffizi. In the spring of 1960, the two scholars decided upon the emergency removal of all the drawings in order to conserve them. At the same time, Barocchi was entrusted with assembling a complete catalogue of the Casa Buonarroti collection, which was also to include the sketches of Michelangelo in the Buonarroti archives. Thanks to Sinibaldi's initiative, the study of Michelangelo's graphic works in the Uffizi was also added "in such a way as to reunite, for ease of consultation, all of the material from the Florentine collections." Still today, the three famous volumes bound in red, published between 1962 and 1964 after monumental research (and from which we

FIG. 8. Michelangelo, *Madonna and Child,* c. 1525, black and red chalk, lead white, and ink on paper. Casa Buonarroti, inv. 71 F.

have extracted the citations for this paragraph), constitute the essential and irreplaceable resource for anyone wishing to understand and deepen his or her knowledge of Michelangelo's graphic works in the Florentine collections.

Thus removed to the prints and drawings room in the Uffizi where they were conserved, the drawings of the collection returned to the Casa Buonarroti only in 1975. In 1960 facsimiles of the Michelangelo drawings were put into the frames and display cases in place of the originals to relieve in some measure what was a traumatic absence. After the large exhibition celebrating the fifth centenary of the birth of Michelangelo and the return of the drawings to Casa Buonarroti, the walls of the museum were again filled with facsimiles. By then old and above all no longer reflecting current museum standards, these copies were substituted in the mid-1980s with the exhibition of Michelangelo originals. But because we now understand the exacting standards of conservation that prohibit the permanent display of graphic works, small groupings from the collection are presented in rotation in a room of the museum outfitted for that purpose.

We happily conclude this account by recalling that the graphic patrimony of the Casa Buonarroti also includes numerous family papers (dating from 1399 to 1815) and many autograph writings of Michelangelo (letters, poems, memoirs, but also drawings), which are now reunited in the 169 volumes of the Buonarroti archives. These archives, too, have undergone a long exile. A nearly century-long sojourn at the Medici Laurentian Library in Florence brought significant reorganization and conservation to the archives during years in which the resources of the Casa Buonarroti were at their limits. For these actions, we must always remain grateful. Yet it is wonderful to note that, a few years ago, when the time seemed right, all the papers were effectively returned to the Casa Buonarroti and placed in an ideal environment that had been prepared for them. Just as in 1975, when director Charles de Tolnay witnessed the return of the drawings of Michelangelo and his school from the Uffizi, so today we can be thankful for the return of the archives. The research we have in progress requires their daily use to understand and clarify family episodes relating to art and history.

But let us return to the affairs of the family and the house. Michelangelo the Younger died in 1647, mourned, as the Florentine writer Filippo Baldinucci observed, "not only by all the virtuous, but by the entire city, to whom his rare qualities were well known." He was succeeded in the governance of the Casa by his nephew, who, according to the tradition of alternating of names, was called Leonardo. A magnanimous caretaker, he succeeded in ensuring that the estate would be preserved intact through ironclad clauses in his will. Upon his death, the palace passed to his son Michelangelo, the probable author of the late seventeenth-century inventory called the *Descrizione buonarrotiana*. After him (we are now at the start of the eighteenth century), ownership reached Filippo Buonarroti (1661–1733), but due to his wide renown rather than the right of primogeniture. A noteworthy antiquarian and archaeologist, he enriched the family collections with Etruscan and Roman works, a complete exhibit of which has been on display in the museum since 1997. With Filippo, the Casa once more became, as in the times of Michelangelo the Younger, a destination for illustrious visitors and saw its final season of splendor.

By contrast, the years bridging the eighteenth and nineteenth centuries were quite difficult both for the palace and the family. In 1799 the Austrian garrison that governed Florence ordered the confiscation of the Buonarroti estate. This happened because the legitimate heir, another Filippo (1761–1837), was a revolutionary and follower of Robespierre, and by then was already in exile in French territory. When Leonardo Buonarroti, son of the eminent Etruscan scholar and antiquarian Filippo whom we have just discussed, conferred the name of his father upon his firstborn, he certainly did not imagine that he would become one of the best-known European revolutionaries of the early nineteenth century, fated to suffer imprisonment and persecution for the communistic theories he held. Filippo took French citizenship in 1793, and became the companion and supporter of Babeuf, participating in the 1796 Conspiracy of Equals. When he died in Paris in 1837, his remains were brought to the cemetery in Montmarte by 1,500 mourners. A considerable bibliography helps us to understand his character in the sense briefly summarized here; less well known, however, are the private affairs of the first years of his life and early manhood. His father, a lieutenant in the *dragoni di stanza* regiment in Pisa, had in fact launched him toward a career befitting a descendant of the Florentine aristocracy, in which the family had been enrolled in 1750. In July 1773 Filippo was named an honorary page of Grand Duke Pietro Leopoldo, and on November 12, 1778, he was vested with the habit of the knights of Santo Stefano and entered into the "caravan of Pisa to fulfill the prescribed four years required to attain seniority," as we read in the entry dedicated to him by Armando Saitta in the *Dizionario biografico degli italiani.* It seems that he was not a model of astuteness or earnestness, inasmuch as he worried his masters. Among them, however, was Angelo Fabbroni, who saw in him a temperament like "a character out of a novel" and "rare talent," and described him as "a Frenchman in the French language, hardly less than a master in music and adequately versed in philosophy"—all endowments that would suit the future that awaited him as a revolutionary, and which seem to be an allusion to the jobs he had to perform in order to support himself, namely as a music and voice instructor and bookseller.

Yet here we must limit ourselves to the implications that are most closely linked to the fate of Casa Buonarroti. When Filippo's father died on November 5, 1799, Florence was going through an especially difficult period, having undergone French occupation just a few months earlier and then garrisoning by Austrian troops. Because none of Leonardo's sons were in the grand duchy at the time of Leonardo's death, "by the terms of the edict of the Florentine Senate of October 2, 1799, concerning the possessions of emigrants, the entire Buonarroti estate was put under sequester and its management entrusted to the hospital of Santa Maria Nuova" (Procacci). Filippo, firstborn son and therefore legitimate heir, had left Tuscany in 1789 and moved to Bastia, where he was joined by his wife, Elisabetta Conti, whom he had married in 1782 and by whom he had four daughters and one son, Cosimo, who was born in Bastia in 1790. Filippo's sale of some of Michelangelo's drawings to Jean-Baptiste Wicar took place during these years, and thus they were removed from the family's collection, as we have seen. Following the demise of the Conspiracy of the Equals, of which he himself had been one of the leaders, Filippo continued to endure imprisonment, confined in the fort on the small island of Pelée opposite Cherbourg while awaiting deportation to Guyana. He was thus permanently barred from contact with his family and country of origin. Meanwhile, Elisabetta, who had returned to Tuscany some years before, succeeded in obtaining the appointment of a guardian for their children and, with the help of other heirs of Leonardo, the annulment of the decree that brought about the sequestration of the family's possessions. When a division of the property among Leonardo's four children was reached on July 31, 1801, the house in Via Ghibellina was allotted to Filippo as firstborn, yet he had to wait in prison for two more years before he was allowed, thanks to Napoleon (who was not yet emperor), to live under supervision in Geneva. He also had to wait until his son, Cosimo, had reached the age of majority so that he could be given responsibility for his father's property. That occurred in 1812, and there had not been any news from Filippo for years. A photograph still preserved in Casa Buonarroti in its beautiful nineteenth-century frame might be an homage of Cosimo, who was then living in the ancestral house, to the memory of his father, with whom he never had any kind of relationship. Mentioned in an inventory of Casa Buonarroti dated 1896, this singular example of filial piety might also demonstrate how the fame of the conspirator and revolutionary had been to some degree accepted and, one could say, treated historically, even by his family.

Cosimo Buonarroti (1790–1858), future minister of public education in the granducal government of Tuscany, thus succeeded in recovering possession of the house in

FIG. 9a, b. Aristodemo Costoli (1803–1871), *Busts of Cosimo Buonarroti and Rosina Vendramin*, before 1857, marble. Casa Buonarroti, inv. 1 & 3.

Via Ghibellina in 1812. By then the palace was in serious decay. A report dated June 10, 1823, prepared by an appraiser to document the improvements that Cosimo had previously made, states that "in 1820 the Casa Buonarroti in Via Ghibellina had practically become a tenement for the lowest class of people." Following major restorations, Cosimo took up residence in the house, marrying, in 1846, the Anglo-Venetian noblewoman Rosina Vendramin (1814–1856), who passionately devoted herself to the cultivation of the family's history and even discovered a sketch model by Michelangelo in the Writing Cabinet. Cosimo died not quite two years after his beloved wife, on February 12, 1858 (fig. 9). Among his last wishes was the appointment of his relative Michelangiolo Buonarroti as caretaker for the new museum operation. Yet on account of the delicate condition of his health, Michelangiolo had to immediately defer to his sister's husband, Angiolo Fabbrichesi, who held the responsibility from the time the house was established as a legal entity (1859) until his death in 1894. In 1865 he published his *Guida della Galleria Buonarroti*, which went through several editions, including one in French.

Although Cosimo's wishes were very clear and there were no direct heirs, upon his death the consignment of the house to the city of Florence was strenuously contested by indirect descendants. Nevertheless, Casa Buonarroti was chartered as a legal entity in 1859 by a decree of Grand Duke Leopoldo di Lorena and confirmed a few months later, following the departure of the grand duke, by the provisional Tuscan government. In this manner, the history of Casa Buonarroti became entwined with the events of the Italian Risorgimento.

The initial management of the legal entity made its showiest presence during the celebrations of the fourth centenary of the birth of Michelangelo, which took place in Florence in 1875. Today Casa Buonarroti preserves numerous records of the event, gathered and displayed in two rooms of the museum. The centenary had an enduring cultural impact on the city and its traditions, from the creation of the Piazzale Michelangelo to the design of the

Tribuna gallery to house the *David*, which was transported in 1873 from the Piazza della Signoria to the Galleria dell'Accademia. In addition, an intricate *sgraffito* decoration for the façade of the palace in Via Ghibellina was contemplated, for which the preparatory drawing survives (fig. 10). Yet financial troubles became so severe that many parts of the palace had to be rented out as private apartments, and in 1881 a decision was made to transfer the collections of antiquities to the Museo Archeologico, where they were destined to remain for more than a century. At the beginning of the twentieth century, Casa Buonarroti housed the Museo Storico-Topografico Fiorentino (Museum of Florentine History and Topography). After World War I, it was again divided up and partially rented out.

The first modern restorations date from 1951. They were performed to honor the aforementioned Giovanni Poggi, who had secured the deposit of not a few works from Florentine galleries for the Casa's museum. An impressive and praiseworthy, even if inevitably dated, restoration took place only upon the occasion of the fourth centenary of the death of Michelangelo in 1964. One of the outcomes of this initiative was the transfer from the Accademia delle Arti del Disegno to Casa Buonarroti of the sole surviving large-scale model by Michelangelo, the *River God* (fig. 11). This moving work can be admired in the museum, standing opposite the wooden model for the façade of San Lorenzo.

The following year, the Ente Casa Buonarroti was incorporated under governmental statutes and the Hungarian scholar Charles de Tolnay named as its director. Tolnay came to Florence from Princeton, having already produced his monumental and well-known biography of Michelangelo. Tolnay continued as director until his death in 1981, pursuing his research on the graphic works of Michelangelo, reorganizing the collections, and adding significant works to the library. Thus we come to the current administration, which, since 1982, with the enlightened aid and support of an active advisory board that has been chaired

FIG. 10. Amos Cassioli, Federigo Andreotti, Niccolò Barabino, Cosimo Conti, Corinto Corinti, Giacomo Roster, *Design for the Sgraffito Decoration for the Façade of Casa Buonarroti*, before 1875. Casa Buonarroti, inv. 667.

by two renowned Michelangelo scholars, first Paola Barocchi and then Luciano Berti, has for many years pursued a scholarly investigation of the history of the institution, which has led, among other things, to a carefully supervised reinstallation of the museum that has been conducted closely along the lines of the early inventories.

The beginning of the third millennium has seen the transformation of Casa Buonarroti into a private foundation, a legal change that happily, owing to the goodwill and cooperation of those involved, has not affected the overall activity of the institution as a museum and as a place of study and research, with an important library open to consultation by researchers and specialists in the bibliography of Michelangelo. Yet inside this building, in addition to reflecting on the events of the past and attending to the conservation of its artistic heritage, we also seek to promote various kinds of external initiatives. Collaborations with several generations of both Italian and foreign scholars, relationships with national and international institutions, daily contact with the papers and works of Michelangelo, and a yearly schedule of by now well-known temporary exhibitions comprise the basic storyline of the enterprise. In recent years these initiatives have led to the comparative study of the life and writings of Michelangelo, including the rarely studied subject of his portraits; a reconsideration of the troubled circumstances of the construction of San Lorenzo and Saint Peter's; and a revisiting of the seventeenth-century history of the Casa and the artworks that so greatly beautify it.

FIG. 11. Michelangelo, *Model for a River God*, c. 1524–27, clay, river sand, animal fur, plant fibers, wood, iron wire, and metallic webbing. Casa Buonarroti, inv. Gallerie 1890, no. 1802.

I

LEONE LEONI (AREZZO 1509–MILAN 1590)

Medal of Michelangelo
1560–61
lead, diameter 2⅜ in. (6.1 cm)
obverse: MICHAELANGELVS· BONARROTVS· FLO· R· AES· ANN· 88 / LEO
reverse: DOCEBO· INIQVOS· V· T· E· IMPII· AD· TE CONVER
inv. 611

On March 14, 1561, Leone Leoni sent a letter to Michelangelo along with four versions, two in silver and two in bronze, of the famous and very beautiful medal that he had dedicated to the great artist, which was designed in Rome and executed in Milan. From another letter sent to Michelangelo about a month later, we learn that Leone was still waiting, with some consternation, for confirmation of their arrival. A probable witness to the preparatory work for the medal survives in an oval medallion portrait in pink wax on a slate base (British Museum, London). On the reverse a cartouche bears an inscription: "Portrait of Michelangiolo Buonarroti made from life by his friend Leone Aretino [Leone Leoni]."

This medal—together with those depicting Pius IV; Gonzalo de Cordova, duke of Sessa; and Francesco d'Avalos, marquis of Pescara (all dating to 1561)—marks one of Leone's last attempts in the art of medal making before he took on an ambitious commission from the Hapsburgs to create monumental bronzes for a chapel at the Escorial complex, near Madrid. Several years later Vasari praised the medal in the Giunti edition (1568) of his *La vita di Michelangelo:* "And at that time Cavalier Leone created a very lively portrait of Michelangelo on a medal and out of kindness to him he fashioned on the reverse a blind man led by a dog [. . .] and because it pleased him so much, Michelangelo gave him a model of a Hercules crushing Antaeus, made by his hand, in wax, with some of his drawings."

On the obverse the medal displays a bust of Michelangelo, in profile, facing right. The legend around the border incorrectly indicates Michelangelo's age as eighty-eight (he was born in 1475). Leone's signature appears at the base of the bust. The reverse depicts an elderly blind man, led by a dog, with a tattered, old-fashioned vest and the trappings of a pilgrim (a cane, waterskin, and rosary). That the physiognomy of the figure clearly recalls the traits of Michelangelo is noted only rarely in the voluminous bibliography on the medal. The biblical passage around the border ("I will teach transgressors your ways, and sinners will be converted to you") is taken from Psalms 51:13.

The meaning of the representation on the reverse is open to debate. Perhaps the least convoluted interpretation, which sees it as an earthly pilgrimage, should be accepted. It seems likely that Michelangelo proposed the subject to Leone, and it was consequently suggested that the blind man with the face of Michelangelo was meant to be understood metaphorically. This hypothesis accords well with a few of Michelangelo's poems about old age (take, for example, the verse "quel ch'altri saggio, me fa cieco e stolto" [what makes others wise, makes me blind and stupid]). From other sources, we know that Leoni kept for himself "many verses," as Giovanni Paolo Lomazzo states in his *Idea del tempio della pittura* (1590).

It should be noted that the description of the reverse contained in Lomazzo's *Trattato dell'arte de la pittura, scoltura et architettura* (1584) differs from the examples known today in the detail of the dog's tight leash: ". . . a medal by a good sculptor, who, on the reverse . . .

BIBLIOGRAPHY

Ernst Steinmann, *Die Portrait-darstellungen des Michelangelo* (Leipzig, 1913), 51–52 (with a large bibliography of preceding works); Giorgio Vasari, *La vita di Michelangelo nelle redazioni del 1550 e del 1568,* ed. Paola Barocchi (Milan, 1962), 1:109, 4:1735–38; Ugo Procacci, *La Casa Buonarroti a Firenze* (Milan, 1965), 209; Giovanni Paolo Lomazzo, "Trattato dell'arte de la pittura, scoltura et architettura" (1584), in *Scritti sulle arti,* ed. Roberto Paolo Ciardi (Florence, 1973–75), 2:162; J. Graham Pollard, "Il medagliere mediceo," in *Gli Uffizi: Quattro secoli di una galleria,* ed. Paola Barocchi and Giovanna Ragionieri (Florence, 1983), 1:281; idem, *Medaglie italiane del Rinascimento nel Museo Nazionale del Bargello* (Florence, 1985), 3:1234–36, no. 719; Gigliola Fragnito, *In museo e in villa. Saggi sul Rinascimento perduto* (Venice, 1988), 194; Philip Attwood, in *The Currency of Fame: Portrait Medals of the Renaissance,* exh. cat., ed. Stephen K. Scher (New York, 1994), 155–57, no. 52; Marina Cano, in *Los Leoni (1509–1608): Escultores del Renacimiento italiano al servicio de la corte de España,* exh. cat., ed. Jesús Urrea (Madrid, 1994), 190–91, no. 43; Eliana Carrara, "Michelangelo, Leone Leoni ed una stampa di Maarten van Heemskerck," *Annali della Scuola Normale Superiore di Pisa* 4, nos. 1–2 (1996): 219–25; Kelley Helmstutler Di Dio, "Leone

where he had portrayed Michel Angelo, had made a poor man led by a dog tied by a cord around his neck, which appeared completely taut and straight like a cane, without any sagging. This allowed even a young boy to manage it and to say that if that dog had pulled that cord so strongly either he would strangle himself or he would not be able to turn in any other direction, to the great humor of a few painters who were with me and who were ready to burst out laughing." The episode most likely dates before 1572, when Lomazzo went blind.

Leone's gift to Michelangelo included, as we have seen, four pieces, two in silver and two in bronze, and the copy in lead displayed here could not have had the same provenance. It is not listed in the old inventories of the Casa Buonarroti and is seldom cited today by specialists. From a technical point of view, one can discern it as an artist's proof. On the other hand, the existence of sixteenth-century versions in lead is attested by the inventory of a collection belonging to Antonio Giganti (1535–1598), a clergyman in the service of prelates and cardinals. Present in the collection were medal impressions in lead, mostly with the images of various famous men, Michelangelo among them. Gigliola Fragnito (1988) has brought attention to the collection inventory.

Given its extraordinary quality, Pollard (1983) believed that the version of the medal in silver, currently preserved in the Museo Nazionale del Bargello, Florence, came into the collections of the Medici as an acquisition from the Buonarroti family.

In the letter of March 14, 1561, Leone alluded to a papal commission, received through the good offices of Michelangelo, that had delayed him in sending the medals. The project, for which he signed a contract on September 12, 1560, was for the tomb of Gian Giacomo de' Medici, the marquis of Marignano, brother of Pius IV. According to Vasari, Leone used a design given to him by Michelangelo for the grandiose monument, which was placed in the right transept of the cathedral of Milan, where it is still today. It is one of the principal testaments to the great fame Leone enjoyed in Milan, which enabled him to build a spectacular home, the Casa degli Omenoni, where Vasari stayed during his 1566 sojourn in the city.

In the section of *Lives of the Artists* dedicated to Leone, Vasari called him "Cavalier Lione sculptor from Arezzo." In 1595, a few years after Leoni's death, Paolo Morigia, in his book on the noble families of Milan (*La nobiltà di Milano*), affirmed that he was born in Menaggio, in the province of Como, to a family from Arezzo. The latter hypothesis was long accepted, even if with some question, but archival research by Kelley Helmstutler Di Dio (1999) has recently demonstrated that Vasari was correct.

P.R.

Aretino: New Documentary Evidence of Leone Leoni's Birthplace and Training," *Mitteilungen des Kunsthistorischen Institutes in Florenz* 43 (1999): 645–52; Jeremy Warren, *Renaissance Master Bronzes from the Ashmolean Museum, Oxford: The Fortnum Collection*, exh. cat. (London, 1999), no. 31; Pina Ragionieri, in *Michelangelo. Grafia e biografia di un genio*, exh. cat. (Milan, 2000), 83, no. 52; idem, *Michelangelo: Drawings and Other Treasures from the Casa Buonarroti, Florence*, exh. cat. (Atlanta, 2001), 42–45, no. 3; Hugo Chapman, *Michelangelo. Drawings: Closer to the Master*, exh. cat. (London, 2005), 263–64, 293, no. 110; Pina Ragionieri, *Michelangelo: The Man and the Myth*, exh. cat. (Syracuse, NY, 2008), 52, no. 4.

2

LEONE LEONI (AREZZO 1509–MILAN 1590)

Letter Written from Milan to Michelangelo in Rome
March 14, 1561
ink on paper, 13 × 8¼ in. (33 × 21 cm)
Archivio Buonarroti, IX, f. 460

The letter can be translated:

My most magnificent and always noteworthy Lord, I am sending to your Lordship by Signor Carlo Visconte—a great man in this city of Milan and beloved by His Holiness—four medals bearing your likeness: two are in silver and the other two in bronze. I would have sent them sooner to your Lordship if I had not been so busy on account of the work that, thanks to your Lordship, I received from His Holiness, and if I had not already trusted that your Lordship would pardon me for the fault of tardiness, though not so for the sin of ingratitude.

The one that is in the case is thoroughly finished, and you will look at it and keep it for love of me. With the other three, you can do what you please, since, for pretense I sent them to Spain and Flanders, and likewise for love I ordered them to be sent to Rome and other parts. I said pretense, because I seem to have acquired and gained too much favor from your Lordship, whom I esteem much; and who would not restrain himself much, since in less than three months I have had two letters from you, divine man, not as a servant of the heart and will, but as a son? But come, I will not trouble your Lordship any more for now, except to ask that you desire to persevere in loving me, and, when necessary, to favor me, and to tell Signor Tommaso del Cavaliere [dei Cavalieri] that I will not forget him. May the Lord give you every happiness, so that I may likewise have happiness.

From Milan, the 14th of March, '61.

From the grateful servant of your Lord, Cavalier Leone.

✝

Molto Mag.co S.r mio sempre oss.mo

Mando a V.S. P. lo S.r Carlo visconte grande suomo in
questa città di Milano, et amato da sua S.tà quattro
medaglie de la vostra effigie, le due saranno d'argento
et saltre due di bronzo. Sarei stato piu prеsto à
mandarle a V.S. se nõ fussi cosi occupato ne lo opera c se
P cagione di V.S. hebbi da sua S.tà et se ancsora
nõ sauessi fede c Sr V.S. mi perdonasse s'errore de
la tardanza, ma nõ gia il peccato de l'ingratitudine
quella c Sr è ms bossolo è tutta rinettata et la guardarò
e c̃o seruarà P amor mio saltre ore ne farà cio c̃se
gli parerà P cioc̃se secõdo c̃sio P ambizione me so mã
date in spagna et in fiandra cõsi P amore ne
torò mãdare a Roma et in altre parte. dissi ambiz̃õ
ne P cioc̃ mi par hauer troppo aquistato a d̃ sauer
guadagnata la gratia di V.S. c̃siu astimo molto
et c̃si nõ si torebbe da molto poi c̃si immeno di
tre mesi so due lettere scritemi da voi suomo diuino
nõ come aseruitor di cuore e di uolontà, ma da fi
gliuolo. t'orsù io nõ darò piu fastidio P hora a
V.S. ecetto c̃se la prego c̃se mi uoglia P seuerar
d'amarmi, et doue occore fauorirmi e a d̃ S.r Tgõa
Thomao del cauall dir c̃sio nõ sarò memorato, il
S.r ui dia ogni contẽza accio io sabbia cõtẽto. Da
Milão il xiiii de Marzo ⅋ 6i.

        D. V.S. ser obligatis.o il cauall Leone

3
DANIELE RICCIARELLI, CALLED DANIELE DA VOLTERRA
(VOLTERRA 1509–ROME 1566)
GIAMBOLOGNA (DOUAI 1529–FLORENCE 1608)

Bust of Michelangelo
1564–66 (head), c. 1600–8 (bust)
bronze, height 23¼ in. (59 cm)
inv. 61

Daniele Ricciarelli, called Daniele da Volterra, was bound to Michelangelo by a long and deep friendship, so much so that he was among the very few who attended him on his deathbed. The profound connection between the two artists no doubt was strengthened by Ricciarelli's extraordinary devotion and by the experience of working together, which resulted in remarkable stylistic affinities. From the mid-1540s, Daniele, who had been in Rome for almost a decade, placed himself in Michelangelo's orbit (confronting the challenging novelties of the *Last Judgment* in the Sistine Chapel) with his important fresco cycles for the Orsini Chapel and the Della Rovere Chapel at Trinità dei Monti. Among the preparatory works for the latter chapel one finds a figurative witness that is particularly touching, the famous cartoon by Daniele (Teylers Museum, Haarlem) which includes a study for the head of an apostle that resembles Michelangelo. Between 1550 and 1556, with the paintings commissioned by Giovanni della Casa—*David and Goliath* (Louvre, Paris), the lost *Aeneas and Dido*, and *Saint John the Baptist* (of which two versions are known, one in Munich and the other in the Pinacoteca Capitolina, Rome)—Ricciarelli began a truly collaborative rapport with the venerable master.

In 1559 Daniele was occupied with work on an equestrian monument of Henry II of France. The king's widow, Catherine de' Medici, had originally commissioned the work from Michelangelo, but by then eighty-five, he was no longer capable of taking on such an enterprise. Thus he gave it to his friend, supplying him with a drawing for the statue, whose dimensions were to challenge those of the statue of Marcus Aurelius in the Campidoglio. He also followed the labors involved in the complex casting, which he did not live to see completed. After Michelangelo's death, on February 18, 1564, Daniele spent the last two years of his own life fulfilling the anything but simple legacy of affections as well as the work left to him by the master. Daniele rented Michelangelo's Roman house, the Macel de' Corvi, in May 1564: "a taking into custody rather than letting out," according to Michelangelo's nephew Leonardo Buonarroti, for whom Daniele was already busy executing a "metal portrait" of Michelangelo based on his death mask. Yet "the labors and hardships" expended on the equestrian monument fatally delayed the portrait's delivery, and as Vasari testifies, they led the artist to his death on April 4, 1566.

At the time of Daniele's death six bronze heads of Michelangelo, not yet properly finished, were found in his workshop, two of which undoubtedly were those meant for Leonardo Buonarroti. After they finally reached Florence, traces of one of them were lost. The other, displaying an indisputably expressive emotional force and early on considered one of the most exalted portraits of Michelangelo, was furnished a few years later with rich drapery created by the Flemish sculptor Giambologna. This contribution led to the attribution of the whole work to Giambologna in a late seventeenth-century inventory of the Casa Buonarroti called the *Descrizione buonarrotiana.*

BIBLIOGRAPHY

Giorgio Vasari, *Le vite de' più eccellenti pittori, scultori e architettori*, ed. Rosanna Bettarini and Paola Barocchi (Florence, 1966–87), 5:547–49; Fabia Borroni Salvadori, "Le esposizioni d'arte a Firenze dal 1674 al 1767," *Mitteilungen des Kunsthistorischen Institutes in Florenz* 18 (1974): 70, 90, 115, 140; Alessandro Cecchi, in Henry A. Millon and Vittorio Magnago Lampugnani, *Rinascimento da Brunelleschi a Michelangelo. La rappresentatione dell'architettura*, exh. cat. (Milan, 1994), 658–59, no. 385 (with preceding bibliography); Eike D. Schmidt, in Sylvia Ferino-Pagden, *Vittoria Colonna: Dichterin und Muse Michelangelos*, exh. cat. (Vienna, 1997), 314–16, no. IV.1; Pina Ragionieri, *Michelangelo: Drawings and Other Treasures from the Casa Buonarroti, Florence*, exh. cat. (Atlanta, 2001), 40–41, no. 2; Alessandro Cecchi, in Vittoria Romani, *Daniele da Volterra, Amico di Michelangelo*, exh. cat. (Florence, 2003), 170–72, no. 54.

In 1767 an exhibition was held in Florence, in the cloister of the church of the Santissima Annunziata, in which the leading Florentine families displayed their treasures. The owner of the Casa Buonarroti at the time, also named Leonardo, participated with two works by Michelangelo—a "low relief in marble" (the *Madonna of the Steps*?) and a "head of woman drawn in black pencil" (the *Cleopatra*?)—together with a *Head of an Old Man*, then attributed to Guido Reni, and the bust of Michelangelo under consideration here, which was still attributed, according to family tradition, to Giambologna.

The dating of the decorative addition of the drapery close to the time of the arrival of the bronze head in Florence was established by Alessandro Cecchi on stylistic grounds in 1994. But returning to the subject on the occasion of a 2003 show at the Casa Buonarroti dedicated to Ricciarelli, Cecchi placed the drapery among Giambologna's final works. In the absence of documentation, we accept this last hypothesis, regarding as not improbable that the embellishment could have originated during the time of Leonardo's son, Michelangelo the Younger, who inherited the family home in 1599 and undertook major renovations and decorations of it.

P.R.

41

4
POMPEO DI GIULIO CACCINI
(FLORENCE 1577–LAST DOCUMENTED 1624)

Michelangelo in His Studio
1595
oil on canvas, 70⅞ × 55⅛ in. (180 × 140 cm)
inv. Gallerie 1890, no. 6306

The creator of this large canvas has not enjoyed the recognition that he undoubtedly deserves. A painter and musician, Caccini "surely contributed to the evolution of sacred iconography in Tuscany between the sixteenth and seventeenth centuries" (Nesi 1997), but he did not enjoy the same fame as others in his family. His father, Giulio Caccini, is remembered in the history of music as a member of the Camerata de' Bardi and a protagonist in the birth of melodrama. His sister Francesca was a celebrated singer as well as a friend of Michelangelo Buonarroti the Younger (the artist's grandnephew) and a frequent guest at the Casa Buonarroti.

The painting, in which mystical references are ritualistically employed to exalt the myth of Buonarroti, is one of several works deposited and put on display at the Casa Buonarroti by Florentine galleries in the 1930s through the initiative of the renowned Michelangelo scholar Giovanni Poggi (1880–1961). For many years, beginning in 1925, he served as Superintendent of Medieval and Modern Art for Tuscany. The transfer document is dated August 13, 1932.

The work can be attributed with certainty to Pompeo di Giulio Caccini on the basis of two documents in the Florentine state archives (verbal communication, Anna Barsanti). The first speaks of a commission made in 1595 by the Accademia dell'Arte del Disegno to Caccini for a painting depicting Michelangelo in the act of braiding three garlands, the symbol of the academy. The second contains the artist's acceptance of the commission. Founded in 1563 by Cosimo I de' Medici on the recommendation of Giorgio Vasari, the academy counted among

its first members Michelangelo himself, who not incidentally was already using as his sign three circles, one within another. In this painting we see him seated, full figure, with his body in profile and his face gazing outward. It is almost as if he is looking at those artists to whom are ideally destined the three garlands he holds in his hand, the symbolic and compositional center of the painting. Allusions to the three arts—painting, sculpture, and architecture—are emphasized in the very faithful reproductions of Michelangelo's masterpieces as painter, sculptor, and architect. His figure occupies an intermediate plane in an idealized surrounding in which a painting on an easel to his right offers a detail of the *Last Judgment*. On the far right, at the top, can be seen a sketch model of a male nude that

BIBLIOGRAPHY

Ernst Steinmann, *Die Portraitdarstellungen des Michelangelo* (Leipzig, 1913), 35, plate 24; Charles de Tolnay, "L'Hercule de Michel-Ange a Fontainebleau," *Gazette des Beaux-Arts* 44 (1964): 135; Ugo Procacci, *La Casa Buonarroti a Firenze* (Milan, 1965), 194, no. 122; Alessandro Nesi, "Inediti documentari e figurativi per Pompeo Caccini," *Erba d'Arno* 68/69 (1997): 56–58, 63, no. 11; idem, "Pompeo Caccini 1613. Il restauro della Madonna del Rosario di San Salvatore a Fucecchio," *Erba d'Arno* 99 (2005): 51; idem, "Bartolomeo Marinari, un pittore sconosciuto del secondo Cinquecento fiorentino," *Paragone*, ser. 3, 57, no. 68 [677] (2006): 82, 86, no. 8.

Workshop of Jacopino del Conte (1510–1598), *Portrait of Michelangelo*, c. 1535. Casa Buonarroti, inv. Gallerie 1890, no. 1708.

enjoyed widespread fame in the sixteenth and seventeenth centuries because it was regarded as an original sketch model for his *David;* critics today recognize it as representing an early cast made from an original by Michelangelo. Another allusion to Michelangelo the sculptor is a copy of the large *Model for a River God* (Casa Buonarroti, see fig. 11, p. 35). In the foreground, lying on the table, is the plan of the Villa Giulia in Rome, upon whose design the artist worked. The few books stacked on the table, together with tools of the trade such as a goose-quill pen, are clear references to Michelangelo the poet.

The face of Michelangelo, as Steinmann (1913) observed, is taken from the best-known and most used prototype, the portrait executed by Jacopino del Conte about 1535.

P.R.

5
CAFAGGIOLO MANUFACTORY

Plate with the Buonarroti Family Coat of Arms
mid-16th century
maiolica, diameter 10⅞ in. (27.7 cm)
inv. 79

The arms of the Buonarroti family appear in the middle of the plate, together with the insignias of the Medici pope Leo X, which were given in 1515 to Michelangelo's brother, Buonarroto Buonarroti, when he was nominated city prior. On that occasion, the pope decided that incumbent priors could insert the blue Medici ball with the lily of France and the letters "L.P.X." (Leo Pontifex X) on the arms of their families.

Since that time, the Buonarroti arms have displayed precisely these attributes. Buonarroto's elevation to prior is depicted in a fresco by Pietro da Cortona in the Room of Night and Day, the second of the seventeenth-century rooms in the Casa Buonarroti.

The plate was executed in the famous maiolica workshop of Cafaggiolo in the Mugello, in the vicinity of Florence. The workshop was installed in the Medici castle of the same name at the end of the fifteenth century.

On the back of the plate can be read, although faded, the mark "SPR," which identified the products of Cafaggiolo for about a century.

P.R.

BIBLIOGRAPHY

Galeazzo Cora, *Storia della maiolica di Firenze e del contado* (Florence, 1973), 37, no. 17; Alessandro Alinari, *Maioliche marcate Cafaggiolo* (Florence, 1987), 35–39; idem, in *Ceramica toscana dal Medioevo al XVIII secolo*, exh. cat., ed. Gian Carlo Boiani (Rome, 1990), 159–60; Pina Ragionieri, *Michelangelo: Drawings and Other Treasures from the Casa Buonarroti, Florence*, exh. cat. (Atlanta, 2001), 38–39, no. 1.

Pietro da Cortona (1596–1669), *Leo X Names Buonarroto Buonarroti a Palatine Count.* Casa Buonarroti, inv. 290.

6

ARTIST OF THE 16TH CENTURY

Madonna of the Steps (after Michelangelo)
c. 1566
bronze, 22½ × 15¾ in. (58 × 40 cm)
inv. 531

This bronze relief reproduces Michelangelo's marble *Madonna of the Steps,* one of his youthful masterpieces housed in the Casa Buonarroti Museum. The marble work, made around 1490, remained in the Via Ghibellina house until Michelangelo's nephew Leonardo gave it as a gift to Duke Cosimo I de' Medici sometime after the death of the artist and before 1568. The bronze casting was in all likelihood made on that occasion. The oldest evidence of the work dates from the late seventeenth century, when it is mentioned, in the inventory known as the *Descrizione buonarrotiana,* as occupying a niche in the Room of the Angels, where it has recently been placed once again. The same room displayed the master's marble relief after Cosimo II returned it to Michelangelo Buonarroti the Younger in 1616. The bronze relief, which still bears its original frame, has traditionally but erroneously been attributed to Giambologna. More recently it has been ascribed—but this proposal also seems unconvincing—to Vincenzo Danti.

P.R.

BIBLIOGRAPHY

Hellmut Wohl, "Two Cinquecento Puzzles," *Antichità viva* 30 (1991): 42–48, no. 6; Giovan Battista Fidanza, *Vincenzo Danti, 1530–1576* (Florence, 1996), 112; Pina Ragionieri, *Michelangelo: Drawings and Other Treasures from the Casa Buonarroti, Florence,* exh. cat. (Atlanta, 2001), 46–47, no. 4.

7

MICHELANGELO

Three Different Lists of Foods
1518
ink on paper, 8⅜ × 5¾ in. (21.3 × 14.5 cm)
Archivio Buonarroti, X, f. 578 verso

While Michelangelo was quarrying marble in Pietrasanta, he jotted down these menus for three different meals on the back of a letter that had been sent to him on March 18, 1518, by Bernardo Nicolini. He used—as he often did, since it was his custom not to waste paper—the first sheet of paper that came to hand. Moreover, the food list, which describes an essential menu for two, four, or six people, shows his scrupulousness in recording the expenses and events of his day-to-day life. It testifies to Michelangelo's frugal way of living, which has often been pointed out by his biographers. The "bochal di tondo" in the last line seems to allow each of the six diners a glass of wine from the vineyards of Colle Tondo, near Serravezza and not far from Pietrasanta.

This note might have been made by the sculptor Pietro Urbano, one of the artist's collaborators. Michelangelo's administrative papers from this period often include notes in Urbano's hand regarding everyday expenses. But the strength and confidence of the handwriting make even these utilitarian notes a typical manifestation of a great artist's genius.

The other annotations read: "Two rolls, a pitcher of wine, a herring; tortelli; a salad, four rolls, a pitcher of wine, a small quarter of a rough wine, a plate of spinach, four anchovies, tortelli; six rolls, two fennel soups, a herring, a pitcher of wine."

P.R.

BIBLIOGRAPHY

Lucilla Bardeschi Ciulich, *Costanza ed evoluzione nella scrittura di Michelangelo*, exh. cat. (Florence, 1989), 28–29, no. 10; idem, *Michelangelo. Grafia e biografia di un genio*, exh. cat. (Milan, 2000), 44; Pina Ragionieri, *Michelangelo: Drawings and Other Treasures from the Casa Buonarroti, Florence*, exh. cat. (Atlanta, 2001), 50–51, no. 6.

pani dua
ü bóchal di vino
una ariga
tortegli

una salata
e quatro pani
ü bo chial di vino
ün quarruccio di brodo
ü piattello di spinaci
quatro a li cei
tortelli

sei pani
dua minestre di finochio
una aringa
ü bochal di tondo

8

MICHELANGELO

Study for the Fortification of the City Gate at the Prato di Ognissanti
1529
red chalk, pen, brown watercolor wash on paper, 15¼ × 22 in. (38.8 × 55.8 cm)
inv. 14 A

BIBLIOGRAPHY

Paola Barocchi, *Michelangelo e la sua scuola. I disegni di Casa Buonarroti e degli Uffizi* (Florence, 1962), 1:136, no. 108, 1:144–45, no. 117; Pietro C. Marani, *Disegni di fortificazioni da Leonardo a Michelangelo*, exh. cat. (Florence, 1984), 80–81, no. 54; Giulio Carlo Argan and Bruno Contardi, *Michelangelo architetto* (Milan, 1990), 145, 202–9; Pina Ragionieri, *Michelangelo: Drawings and Other Treasures from the Casa Buonarroti, Florence*, exh. cat. (Atlanta, 2001), 114–15, no. 30.

At the beginning of 1529, alarming news was spreading throughout Florence: Medici pope Clement VII was making plans to return his family to power with the help of the imperial army. The Medici had been driven out of the city two years earlier on May 17. In response, the Governo Popolare (the "popular" or civil government) decided to complete the defensive works that had been started in 1526 but left unfinished while the city was still under Medici rule. The Committee of Nine on Military Affairs (Nove della Milizia) was formed, and Michelangelo was called to take part. Shortly thereafter, he would be named "governor and procurator general of the fortifications." Charged with this important responsibility, encouraged by the regard of his fellow citizens, and steadfast in his faith in republican government, Michelangelo proceeded to work out a series of proposals to defend the gates of the city walls. But, on account of their complexity and novelty, they were either never built or were constructed only partially and since destroyed. The identification of these schemes was therefore possible only through the study of the extraordinary drawings kept in the Casa Buonarroti collection. The fortification plans were known to the court of Louis XIV, having been studied by the marquis of Vauban, and were then variously cited up until the beginning of the twentieth century, yet it was not until rather more recently that they came to be fully recognized and appreciated.

Despite the brief duration of the glorious and ephemeral second Florentine republic (1527–30), the fortification plans Michelangelo designed for the defense of the city bear witness to several stages in his thinking. An initial grouping of sheets reveals some uncertainties and an analysis that had not yet been fully developed, either from a stylistic point of view or a functional one—a situation that makes it difficult to determine which of the eleven city gates the artist was working on. More imaginative motifs followed shortly thereafter that were more precisely gauged to the purpose of fortification—motifs that the drawing shown here wonderfully illustrates. Here the splendid "star" of the bulwark is securely placed in the moat created by the deviated stream of the Mugnone with a striking originality and a dynamic talent that is fully consistent with Michelangelo's architecture of the period. To experts, the tactical and strategic novelties in sheets like these appear undeniable, possessing a potential operational validity that the artist's contemporaries no doubt were not able to discern.

Argan's hypothesis (1990) is impressive in this regard, along with the completely plausible historical-political assessment that follows from it: "The twenty-eight drawings of bastions in Casa Buonarroti almost seem like an incredible event from beyond time, charged with blazing fury and explosive energy. They are just building plans, but they should not be regarded as preparatory studies made in view of some future construction. [Michelangelo] knew that they would never be built; there was neither the time nor the will. . . . It would nevertheless be an

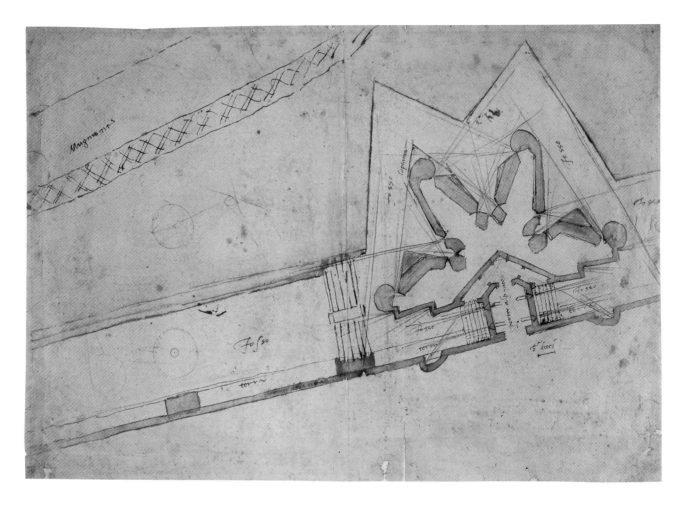

The city gate at Prato di Ugnissanti in Florence, from the "Chain Map," c. 1472.

error to consider those drawings as a sort of intellectual adventure composed in a state of patriotic excitement yet substantially isolated in the progress of his architectural work."

On the back of the drawing, a note in Michelangelo's hand carries the date July 25, 1528. That the front of the sheet is dated to the following year, linked as it is to historical circumstances, is not surprising if one bears in mind how paper was used and reused at the time, even after long intervals.

P.R.

9
MICHELANGELO
Study for a Resurrected Christ
1532–33
black chalk on paper, 15 × 9⅞ in. (38.1 × 25.2 cm)
inv. 61 F

In the collection of drawings by Michelangelo in the Casa Buonarroti, this nude study stands out for its extraordinary expressiveness. Today, scholars almost unanimously recognize it as an autograph work; the few distinguished negative opinions concerning its attribution belong to the past, such as the assessments of Popp (1922), Berenson (1938), and Dussler (1959).

The drawing was considered an early concept for the Christ in the *Last Judgment*, which, occupying the wall behind the altar in the Sistine Chapel, was executed by Michelangelo between 1535 and 1541. Already in the distant past, on the occasion of the Michelangelo centenary in 1875, both Fabbrichesi (the author of a guide to the Buonarroti gallery, which had been open to the public for no more than fifteen years) and Gotti (in his *Vita di Michelangelo*, which in its time enjoyed well-deserved fame) pointed to our drawing as a study for the Sistine wall. The drawing was again linked to the *Last Judgment* in 1938 by Berenson, who otherwise refuted the attribution to Michelangelo. But that hypothesis lost credibility among scholars closer to our time, who, following the lead of studies by Johannes Wilde, placed this sheet between 1532 and 1533, among the group of preparatory drawings for a *Resurrection of Christ*, which, according to Wilde, occupied Michelangelo's attention for a rather long time. In his thorough analysis, Wilde lists some fourteen drawings that he believed to be unquestionably autograph and surely related to the theme of the Resurrection.

The intended site for Michelangelo's studies on this theme is unknown. Michael Hirst's suggestion is fascinating; he connects these drawings to the complex decoration of the Chigi Chapel in the church of Santa Maria della Pace in Rome, which Raphael had begun in the second decade of the sixteenth century. According to Hirst, Michelangelo would have supplied graphic models to the Venetian painter Sebastiano del Piombo (c. 1485–1547), with whom he had been friends for more than a decade, as a basis for the chapel's altarpiece. Among the legends founded in truth about the artist, in fact, was the manner in which he displayed generosity to friends: from his early youth, we see him busy supplying cartoons or models to whomever was around him, whether important

BIBLIOGRAPHY

Angiolo Fabbrichesi, *Guida della Galleria Buonarroti* (Florence, 1875), 10; Angiolo Gotti, *Vita di Michelangelo* (Florence, 1875), 2:192; Johannes Wilde, *Italian Drawings in the Department of Prints and Drawings in the British Museum: Michelangelo and His Studio* (London, 1953), 87–91; Michael Hirst, "The Chigi Chapel in Santa Maria della Pace," *Journal of the Warburg and Courtauld Institutes* 24 (1961): 161–85; Paola Barocchi, *Michelangelo e la sua scuola. I disegni di Casa Buonarroti e degli Uffizi* (Florence, 1962), 170–71, no. 137; Michael Hirst, *Michel-Ange dessinateur*, exh. cat. (Paris and Milan, 1989), 96–99; Flavio Fergonzi, in *Michelangelo nell'Ottocento. Rodin e Michelangelo*, exh. cat., ed. Maria Mimita Lamberti and Christopher Riopelle (Milan, 1996), 174–75, no. 40; Pina Ragionieri, *Michelangelo: Drawings and Other Treasures from the Casa Buonarroti, Florence*, exh. cat. (Atlanta, 2001), 136–37, no. 36.

Michelangelo, *Study for a Resurrected Christ*. Casa Buonarroti, inv. 61 F, verso.

artists, from Piombo to Pontormo, or minor figures, to whom he was nevertheless bound by relationships of mild benevolence.

In our drawing, Michelangelo appears occupied in the study of complex compositional modules that only later would attain the plastic power and boldness of the *Last Judgment*. Here he captured the dynamic force of a body seized in the moment when it is ready to pivot upon itself, a posture that is also seen in another study on the same subject in the Casa Buonarroti collection (inv. 66 F), which is more or less contemporaneous. A unique, communicative immediacy and a delicate and barely implied chiaroscuro distinguish the work. The dramatic superimposition of pentimenti, focusing here upon the movement of the legs, beautifully conveys the artist's changes and rethinkings.

On the back of the sheet, a brilliant study seems to represent a variant in reverse of the figure on the front.

P.R.

10

FLORENTINE ARTIST OF THE 16TH CENTURY
Male Torso
c. 1540
terracotta, height 9 in. (23 cm)
inv. 539

This *bozzetto* (preliminary model) is seen today without a head or arms, and the thighs are cut off just below the groin. The upper limbs and head became detached when the model was fired, as indicated by the dark stains, similar to burns, which are visible along the fragmented areas.

The torso, characterized by its strong shape, is curved forward and slightly pushed to the left by a movement of the right arm, which seemingly crosses the chest, forcing it into a slight twist. The head was probably turned to the right, as indicated by the muscular tension of the neck and the orientation of what remains of the chin. The left thigh is slightly forward and bears the weight of the body. The vigorous musculature of the chest finds a corresponding resonance in the back, where a powerful anatomical study underlines the curve imposed on the back by the depth of the spinal column.

Jeannine O'Grody (1999) has observed a series of subtle lines scratched across the torso, running vertically from the chest to the thighs along the right and left sides of the front and the back. These lines would have been scratched, according to O'Grody, during the final phase of bronze casting, when the mold was detached from the model. This *bozzetto* would therefore represent one for a bronze that today is lost. This interpretation, which would explain the smoothness of the surface of the torso, finds a basis in the well-grounded sixteenth-century practice of making bronze castings both from ancient statuary and from sculptures by Michelangelo and other contemporary masters.

Iconographically, the figure—which strongly recalls the *Belvedere Torso* (like many other busts from Michelangelo's circle)—has frequently been identified as a study for one of the *Slaves* on the tomb of Julius II. Yet in reality, as Shell (1992) has pointed out, there is no connection between the *bozzetto* and the marble sculptures. Goldscheider (1962), on the other hand, suggested that the torso be regarded as a model that Michelangelo would have used to create one or more figures for the *Last Judgment*. Yet the monumentality and massiveness of the bodies on the Sistine wall are not found in the anatomy of the *bozzetto*, which seems rather distant from the hand of Michelangelo, especially in the execution of the rigid and swollen musculature of the back.

In any case, the attribution of this model to Michelangelo has never achieved sizeable scholarly consensus. The nineteenth-century inventories of the Casa Buonarroti (1859, 1880, 1896) and Fabbrichesi, in the successive editions of his guide to the gallery (1865, 1875, 1886), always and only described the work as a male torso in clay or dark terracotta, without attribution. Even Thode (1913) did not put forward any theory about the origin of the work; nor did Tolnay (1954), who, while appreciating its fine quality, pointed out the difference in execution with respect to other models by Michelangelo on account of its "more finished" appearance. By contrast, Goldscheider (1953) and Procacci (1965) discerned the hand of Michelangelo in the *bozzetto*. With the exception of Carlo Falciani (1998), who recently attributed it to Pontormo,

BIBLIOGRAPHY

Henry Thode, *Michelangelo. Kritische Untersuchungen über seine Werke* (Berlin, 1913), 3:281, no. 592; Charles de Tolnay, *Michelangelo* (Princeton, 1954), 4:157, no. 4; Ludwig Goldscheider, *Michelangelo: Painting, Sculpture, Architecture* (London, 1953), 273; idem, *Michelangelo's Bozzetti for Statues in the Medici Chapel* (London, 1957); idem, *A Survey of Michelangelo's Models in Wax and Clay* (London, 1962), n. pag.; Ugo Procacci, *La Casa Buonarroti a Firenze* (Milan, 1965), 189; Orietta Rossi Pinelli, *Chirurgia della memoria: scultura antica e restauri storici*, in *Memoria dell'antico nell'arte italiana*, ed. S. Settis (Turin, 1986), 3:181–250; Vincenzo Farinella, in *Michelangelo e l'arte classica*, exh. cat., ed. G. Agosti and V. Farinella (Florence, 1987), 54–63; Anna Maria Massinelli, *Bronzi e anticaglie nella Guardaroba di Cosimo I*, exh. cat. (Florence, 1991), 63–73; Janice Shell, in *The Genius of the Sculptor in Michelangelo's Work*, exh. cat., ed. P. Marani (Montreal, 1992), 220–21; Gianni Papi, *Andrea Commodi* (Florence, 1994), 150–52; Carlo Falciani, "Alcuni disegni, e 'modelli di terra bellissimi,'" *Artista* (1998): 84–98; Jeannine A. O'Grody, "'Un semplice modello': Michelangelo and His Three-dimensional Preparatory Works," PhD diss., Case Western Reserve University, 1999, 270–72; Elena Lombardi, in *I bozzetti michelangioleschi della Casa Buonarroti* (Florence, 2000), 54–59.

today the *bozzetto* is seen as a work of a
Florentine sculptor of the sixteenth century
and associated with that particular climate in
Florence of the 1530s and 1540s in which art
ists, after Michelangelo's final departure for
Rome, continued more than ever to study the
works, drawings, and models that the master
had left in his studio in Via Mozza or that
were still seen in the workshop of the New
Sacristy of San Lorenzo.

E.L.

Apollonios of Athens,
Belvedere Torso, 1st cen-
tury B.C., marble. Vatican
Museums, Museo Pio-
Clementino, Rome.

11

MICHELANGELO

Letter Written in Rome to His Nephew Leonardo In Florence
December 28, 1563
ink on paper, 11⅝ × 8½ in. (29.5 × 21.5 cm)
Archivio Buonarroti, IV, f. 182

> *Leonardo, I received your last letter with twelve beautiful and good little marzolino*
> *cheeses. I thank you for them and delight in your well being, and it is the same for me.*
> *And having received more letters from you in the past, and not having replied, I failed*
> *because my hand was not working. Yet from now on I will have others write for me*
> *and I will sign. Nothing else is happening on my end.*
>
> *From Rome, 28 December 1563*
> > I, Michelagniolo Buonarroti
>
> *To Leonardo di Buonarroto Simoni in Florence*

BIBLIOGRAPHY

Il carteggio di Michelangelo,
ed. Paola Barocchi and Renzo
Ristori (Florence, 1965–83),
5:311, no. MCCCXCI; *Il
carteggio indiretto di Michelangelo,* ed. Paola Barocchi,
Kathleen Loach Bramanti,
and Renzo Ristori (Florence,
1988–95), 2:172–73, no. 358.

The last letter that Michelangelo wrote in his own hand to his favorite nephew, less than two months before his death, is a final testament to the long correspondence comprising, on the part of the uncle, advice, reproaches, and shared affection. It is cited with feeling for the gratitude it expresses over the modest gift of delicately flavored little cheeses, and especially for the emotions aroused by the phrase "Nothing else is happening on my end." A stock phrase found not infrequently in letters of the time, it appears here loaded with a sense of abandonment and isolation, coming at the end of a letter in which nothing in fact happens. It reflects a kind of loneliness that biographers and scholars of Michelangelo have done little to probe—the simple, inescapable solitude of old age.

Handwriting that is still clear and sharp, yet descending toward the bottom of the page, characterizes the few lines, which truly are of special biographical significance because they contain the sad prediction of the artist that from that time forward he will only be able to sign messages written for him by others. Indeed, the next letter from Rome to reach Leonardo, six weeks later (February 14, 1564), carried alarming news. Written in the hand of Michelangelo's faithful friend Daniele da Volterra, the letter was sent by Diomede Leone, who, along with Tommaso dei Cavalieri and Daniele, aided Michelangelo during the last months of his life. In an accompanying note, Leone sketched an affectionate portrait of the ailing man, who still did not want to give up his daily habits: "A short time ago I left him sitting up, conscious and sensible, but very much weighed down by continual drowsiness; which, in order to chase it away . . . he wanted to try going for a ride on horseback, according to his usual custom every evening when the weather is good; but the cold of the season and the feebleness of his mind and legs prevented him, and thus he returned to sit by the fire, propped up in a chair, where he is much happier to stay than in bed."

Michelangelo had only four more days to live when he appended a weak, irregular, and hard-to-decipher signature to the February letter. He was signing with his own hand his wish to see his nephew one last time. But we know that it did not happen that way: by the time Leonardo reached Rome, his famous uncle had been dead for a few days, and solemn funeral rites had been held in his honor at the church of Santi Apostoli. The lone heir thus put into action his famous plan to steal the corpse. As we know from Vasari, once the body had been transported to Florence disguised as "merchandise," the city and its artists paid tribute to the artist in San Lorenzo before giving him final burial in Santa Croce.

P.R.

Leonardo ebbi la tua ultima cō dodici marzolini begli e buo
ni e me ne rigratio rallegrādomi dello uostro buono essere
eh simile eh io e auendo riceuuto pel passato piu tua
e no auēdo risposto e mācato p che la mano no mi serue
po da ora inanzi farō scriuere altri e io sotto scriuerō
altro no machadero di Roma adi 28 di dicēbro 1563

Jo michelagniolo
buonarroti

TIBERIO TITI (FLORENCE 1573–1627)

*Preliminary Study for "Placing the Bust of Michelangelo
on the Artist's Tomb in Santa Croce"*
1618–20
oil on canvas, 14⅝ × 13⅝ in. (37 × 34.5 cm)
inv. G.A.A., no. 7486

This is the only known preliminary version of a work commissioned by Michelangelo Buonarroti the Younger for the four seventeenth-century rooms in the Casa Buonarroti. Tiberio Titi received the commission in 1615, and documents show that the prepared canvas was taken to the artist's workshop on September 19 of that year. The first payment was made in August 1618, but the finished canvas was delivered only two years later, to be inserted in one of the ceiling panels of the Gallery, the first of the four rooms, where it can still be seen today.

Son of the painter and architect Santi di Tito, Tiberio Titi began his career, in keeping with the custom of his time, as an apprentice in his father's workshop. He soon became his father's active collaborator, and his small paintings on copper were well known. In these works (which are lost today), the artist recounted famous scenes from history and myth. Even in painted works of larger dimensions, Titi often turned to historical themes as well as to sacred subjects. A renowned portraitist, he was in demand at the Medici court and indeed worked there actively in the 1620s, until the arrival of the Flemish portraitist Justus Suttermans made Titi's style appear old-fashioned. One of Titi's best-known portraits is that of the newborn Leopoldo de' Medici (1617, Palazzo Pitti, Florence), the future cardinal whose famous collection would include a large number of Titi's miniature portraits. Michelangelo the Younger commissioned the canvas in question while the artist was still playing a role of great importance at court.

The canvas highlights the salient characteristics of Titi's style. Light illuminates the figures from the side, the source being to the left and high up, strongly suggesting the influence of Caravaggio. Considering its location in the Gallery—the room where a singular biography of Michelangelo is told through pictures— the painting also reveals Titi's passion for history. And the event recorded in his painting is a historical episode— the erection of a funeral monument to Michelangelo in the church of Santa Croce—frozen here in the moment when the bust of the artist is raised on the tomb.

Michelangelo died in his Roman residence Macel de' Corvi on February 18, 1564. His nephew and sole heir Leonardo did not arrive until several days later, by which time his celebrated uncle had already been honored by a state funeral in the church of Santi Apostoli.

BIBLIOGRAPHY

Ugo Procacci, *La Casa Buonarroti a Firenze* (Milan, 1965), 176; Massimo Vezzosi, in *Arte in Toscana dal XV al XVIII secolo. Dipinti, disegni, sculture presentati da Massimo Vezzosi* (Florence, 1995), 40–42; Pina Ragionieri, *Michelangelo: Drawings and Other Treasures from the Casa Buonarroti, Florence*, exh. cat. (Atlanta, 2001), 61–62, no. 11.

Tiberio Titi, *Placing the Bust of Michelangelo on the Artist's Tomb in Santa Croce*, 1615–20, oil on canvas. Casa Buonarroti, inv. 236.

Leonardo famously undertook the theft of the body, which he removed to Florence, as we learn from Vasari, disguised as "merchandise." There Michelangelo was honored by artists as well as the city in the church of San Lorenzo before finding a final resting place in Santa Croce. The solemn funerary monument devoted to his memory was erected by Grand Duke Cosimo I de' Medici but carried out at Leonardo Buonarroti's expense. In the present canvas Titi's skill as a portraitist is evident in his depictions of Leonardo with his wife, Cassandra Ridolfi, and two of their young children; one of them, Michelangelo the Younger, the commissioner of the artwork, is shown as six years old, his age in 1574, the year of the scene being represented.

This oil sketch appears carefully executed and properly finished, further evidence of the attention with which Michelangelo the Younger oversaw the setting up and decoration of the four Casa Buonarroti rooms. The portrayal of the family group is an indication of his filial piety. The changes that can be noted from the preliminary to the finished work are, in all probability, the result of precise "advice" given by him: for instance, in the final work, the figure in the left foreground, contrary to the first version, has a bare back and is capless; in this way, his curly hair and the muscles of his torso capture a brighter beam of light.

P.R.

13, 14
BENEDETTO CALENZUOLI (FLORENCE)
BASED ON A DESIGN BY PIETRO DA CORTONA
(CORTONA 1596–ROME 1679)
Two-panel Door with Allegorical Figures (Poetry and History)
1641–42
wood inlay and mother of pearl, 71¼ × 36¼ in. (181 × 92 cm),
   71¼ × 27½ in. (181 × 70 cm)
inv. 213, 220

These panels are part of a series of six rare and refined double-panel doors commissioned by Michelangelo Buonarroti the Younger at the conclusion of the laborious project that he had initiated in 1612 to decorate the palace in Via Ghibellina. The doors, which remain in place today, were mounted to grace the thresholds of the Gallery, the first of the sumptuous seventeenth-century rooms whose painted and sculptural decorations were intended to exalt Michelangelo's genius. The twelve panels are arranged in pairs to make four doors and to close two wall closets.

The great painter Pietro da Cortona was Michelangelo the Younger's guest while he worked, with some interruptions, from 1641 to 1647 on the decoration of the Palazzo Pitti, commissioned from Grand Duke Ferdinand II de' Medici in 1637. The attribution of the design to him is based on the *Descrizione buonarrotiana* inventory, dated 1684: "by Pietro da Cortona . . . the doors from the first room of the Gallery equally decorated with figures represented in various inlaid woods, made by Benedetto Calenzuoli, an errand boy for a woodworker at the time, with the help of Michelangelo Buonarroti, junior." Pietro's contribution was confirmed by Francesco Baldinucci at the beginning of the eighteenth century. The passage from the inventory points to the scant reputation of the inlayer and the significance of the commissioner's involvement. Michelangelo the Younger—and many files in the Buonarroti archives bear this out—devoted the greatest attention to the design and decoration of the four seventeenth-century rooms. His involvement was not limited to the selection of the artists but included a scrupulous elaboration of the iconographic programs. He was not new to such undertakings; outside the walls of his home, the design of the images that decorate the Sala della Stufa in Florence's Palazzo Pitti, a masterpiece in fresco by Pietro da Cortona begun in 1637, can be traced back to him.

Documents preserved in the Buonarroti archives tell us that from June through December of 1641 the veneer in walnut and orange for the doors of the Gallery was completed, and it is therefore likely that the panels were installed in 1642. The inlays were executed primarily in walnut with a precision that attests to the involvement of the patron of the house. Principal details are in orange-tree wood, light yellow in color, with insets in mother of pearl. The figures depicted, both in these examples and others in the series, are characterized by lengthened proportions, reflecting a still mannerist taste, and fantastic head coverings, halfway between the Florence of Buontalenti and that of Callot. Even today the subject matter has not been completely clarified. In fact, the twelve characters depicted in the panels do not seem to correspond either to the seven liberal arts or to the nine muses. Attempts to determine at least the gender of the figures have not produced definitive answers.

It is certain, however, that these panels contain female figures, with allegories that align with others in other media present in the room dedicated to the glory of the great ancestor.

BIBLIOGRAPHY

Adriaan W. Vliegenthart, *La Galleria Buonarroti. Michelangelo e Michelangelo il Giovane* (Florence, 1976), 220–25; Roberto Contini, in *Case di artisti in Toscana,* ed. Roberto Paolo Ciardi (Florence, 1998), 151–65.

The door related to Poetry depicts two women: the one on the left holds a trumpet in her hand, and the one on the right clutches a viol and a scroll — attributes that harmonize with the figures in Cesare Ripa's *Iconologia*, the highly successful manual of visual symbols, published for the first time without images in Rome in 1593 and reprinted many times thereafter with accompanying illustrations.

The door associated with History shows on its left panel a woman with a parchment; on the right, a female figure holds in her hands a quill pen and an inkwell. The parchment, quill, and inkwell are generic elements that could refer to many disciplines. But one arrives at the theme accepted here because these attributes do not oppose any such identification, and especially because Michelangelo the Younger was strongly interested in historical subjects and often engaged in historical research.

P.R.

15

Model of the Cart for the Transport of David

1873

wood, iron, and plaster, 18½ × 13½ × 13⅝ in.

(47 × 34.5 × 34.7 cm)

inv. 698

The removal of the statue of *David* from Piazza della Signoria to the Accademia di Belle Arti in Florence took place between July 31 and August 4, 1873, using a cart designed by the engineers Francesco Porra and Giuseppe Poggi. Casa Buonarroti possesses an accurate and original model of this vehicle. The statue was placed in the cart in an upright position, with the lower part enclosed by a wooden crate fixed to the base, a knee, and the upper legs. A suspension system of strong steel springs guarded against shocks. The cart moved on tracks and had a special rotating bed to allow it to negotiate street corners. The equipment itself was made in the railway workshops of the Strade Ferrate Romane. The move took five days, as the heat of the season made work possible only from four to eleven in the morning. The move, prompted by well-founded worries about the conservation of the statue, was perhaps the first case of the removal of a work of art from an outdoor location for such reasons. It is worth recalling that an imperfection in the marble block from which the statue was sculpted had been noticed as early as December 1505, when the location of the recently finished work was being decided. In fact, the possibility of placing it under the shelter of the Loggia dei Lanzi in Piazza della Signoria was considered. But *David* was set up in front of Palazzo Vecchio, where it suffered damage on several occasions, including from a lightning strike and as the target of street violence, sometimes politically motivated.

The task of finding a suitable protected location for the colossal masterpiece was intensified by the fact that it had always been seen as a paragon of beauty and a sublime symbol of the city. As early as 1846, Marchese Nerli, head of the corps of civil engineers in Tuscany, had proposed moving the statue and replacing it with a "cast in bronze, to be commissioned from the royal founder Clemente Papi." The plan, considered too expensive at the time, was taken up again five years later by Nerli's successor, Alessandro Manetti, who detected in the statue "noticeable signs of degradation such as to arouse serious concern over its safety, especially if any earthquake shock should occur, even a slight one." The old proposal of the Loggia dei Lanzi was revived but rejected because of the statue's size. Once again the project came to a standstill, and for more than ten years *David* remained where it was, but with a roof to protect it from the weather. In the meantime, Clemente Papi had made the cast bronze copy that would be erected on a monumental base in the middle of Piazzale Michelangelo in 1875. Finally, a commission established in 1866 proposed various homes for *David*, including the grand salon of the recently opened Museo del Bargello and two different locations inside the complex of San Lorenzo. Eventually, the choice fell on the Accademia di Belle Arti, where, in 1875, *David* was the centerpiece of the most important exhibition staged to celebrate Michelangelo's fourth centenary. The statue found its definitive home in 1882, in the Tribuna gallery designed and built especially for it by architect Emilio De Fabris.

P.R.

BIBLIOGRAPHY

Aurelio Gotti, *Vita da Michelangelo Buonarroti narrata con l'aiuto di nuovi documenti* (Florence, 1875), 2:35–51; Giorgio Vasari, *La vita di Michelangelo nelle redazioni del 1550 e del 1568*, ed. Paola Barocchi (Milan/Naples, 1962), 2:204–8; Stefano Corsi, in *Michelangelo nell'Ottocento—il centenario del 1875*, exh. cat. (Milan, 1994), 36, no. 10.

16

ARTIST OF THE 19TH CENTURY

The Casa Buonarroti
c. 1839
hand-colored lithograph, 5½ × 7½ in. (14 × 19 cm)
inv. 554

The lithograph shows the Casa Buonarroti as it appeared in the first half of the nineteenth century, when the last of the Buonarroti, Cosimo (1790–1858), had already undertaken major renovations. Of note are the iron grates on the ground floor, which a municipal ordinance of 1873 later required to be modified, judging them dangerous because they protruded too far. At the bottom of the lithograph, there is an inscription that already testifies to the touristic success of the home: "View of the Home of Michelangelo Buonarroti / Florence, Via Ghibellina No. 7588." This splendid item was donated to the Casa Buonarroti in 1970 by Baron Basile de Lemmerman.

P.R.

BIBLIOGRAPHY

Ugo Procacci, *La Casa Buonarroti a Firenze* (Milan, 1965), 46 and figure E; Charles de Tolnay, *L'omaggio a Michelangelo di Albrecht Dürer* (Rome, 1972), 15.

Veduta della casa di Michelangelo Buonaroti Firenze via Ghibellina N.º7588

FIG. 1. The Sistine Chapel, interior.

Public and Private

IN THE SISTINE CHAPEL

Gary M. Radke

WHEN MICHELANGELO CREATED HIS FAMOUS FRESCOES for the ceiling and altar wall of the Sistine Chapel (fig. 1), he was well aware that the chapel's form and decoration reflected the personal and institutional concerns of popes and artists who had come before him. He also knew that the Sistine Chapel was a uniquely public and private space. It served as the pope's private palace chapel and the site of secret conclaves that selected new popes. At the same time, the pope welcomed laity and religious to visit the chapel both during and outside ceremonial occasions. Michelangelo, then, could not presume a single audience for his work. Nor could he indulge in purely personal or idiosyncratic expression. He had to consider how his work might relate to what had preceded him and how to address different audiences. Working in the Sistine Chapel challenged Michelangelo to create works that were complex and yet readily intelligible, novel but historically attuned, personal and universal: in other words, both public and private.

Pope Sixtus IV (1471–84) began building the chapel in 1477, when Michelangelo was just two years old and more than thirty years before Sixtus's nephew, Pope Julius II (1503–13), would ask him to paint the ceiling. The Sistine Chapel replaced the so-called Cappella Magna (great or large chapel) of the thirteenth-century Vatican Palace, which had fallen into considerable disrepair during the century-long exile of the papacy in Avignon. Pope Nicholas V (1447–55) began reclaiming the Vatican and fortifying its hillside site in the mid-fifteenth century, but times were still unsettled, so Sixtus's architect—perhaps the little documented Baccio Pontelli or Giovannino de' Dolci, whose son received part payment for some construction work in 1486—fashioned a militarily inspired structure (fig. 2). The chapel originally loomed like a watchtower over the papal apartments, the crenellated balcony at its roof line affording practical as well as symbolic defense for an embattled papacy. But the great height of the chapel's sheer walls and insufficient foundations led to large cracks forming on the ceiling and walls, necessitating the construction of wall buttresses. The structural consolidation opened an opportunity for Pope Julius to ask Michelangelo to replace Sixtus's vault decorations.

FIG. 2 The Sistine Chapel, exterior.

Though Michelangelo complained vociferously about receiving the commission—he did not wish to be taken off a spectacular papal tomb project and feared that his rivals Bramante and Raphael had convinced the pope to offer him the painting project to embarrass him—there were few more prestigious sites of papal patronage (see cat. no. 17). Sixtus commissioned the leading painters of his day to adorn the walls and ceiling. Marble workers inlaid the floor and fashioned a choir screen and loft; woodworkers carved and inlaid doors and benches; embroiderers, illuminators, and goldsmiths crafted liturgical garments and vessels, hangings, candelabra, and service books; composers and singers filled the chapel with extraordinary music; and preachers gave learned sermons. The very proportions of the space called for comparison with Solomon's temple in Jerusalem: the length of each structure was twice its height and three times its width.

Papal majesty and ceremony required that the chapel be not only splendid but highly functional (fig. 3). Patterns on the inlaid marble floor clearly mark and delineate the space. A central strip of interlocking circles marches from the entrance to the choir screen, which bisects the space. Papal bodyguards stood watch along this route, forcing lay visitors to the

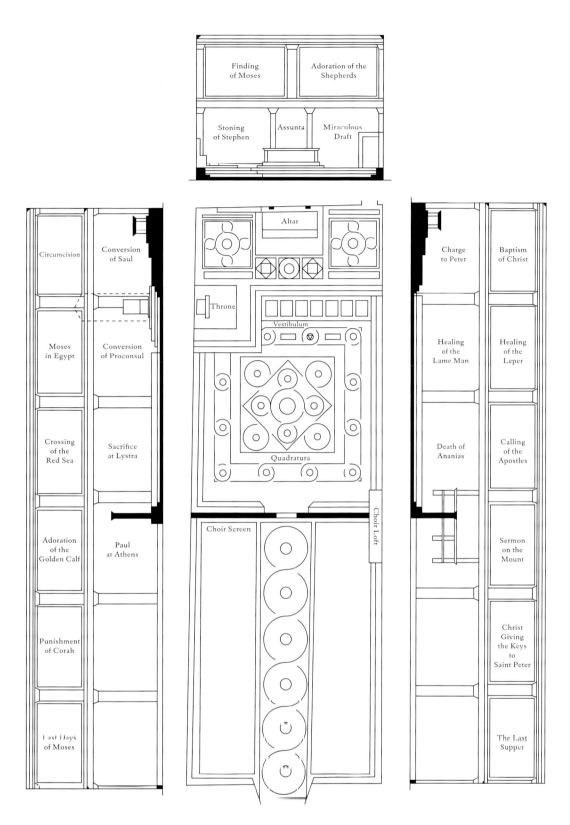

Finding of Moses

Adoration of the Shepherds

Stoning of Stephen

Assunta

Miraculous Draft

Altar

Circumcision

Conversion of Saul

Charge to Peter

Baptism of Christ

Throne

Vestibulum

Moses in Egypt

Conversion of Proconsul

Healing of the Lame Man

Healing of the Leper

Crossing of the Red Sea

Sacrifice at Lystra

Death of Ananias

Calling of the Apostles

Quadratura

Adoration of the Golden Calf

Paul at Athens

Sermon on the Mount

Choir Screen

Choir Loft

Punishment of Corah

Christ Giving the Keys to Saint Peter

Last Days of Moses

The Last Supper

sides. During repeated entrances and exits into the chapel, the pope stopped on a large porphyry disk at the door. Its material, which marked the position of similar ceremonial pauses in ceremonies at papal basilicas throughout Rome, signaled the imperial power and status of the papacy, which the popes traced back to Constantine, the first Christian emperor. It also marked the ideal vantage point for viewing the entire chapel, which Michelangelo later took into account as he laid out Old Testament scenes on the ceiling and imagined the cataclysmic effects of the Last Judgment on the altar wall.

FIG. 3. Plan of the Sistine Chapel. Redrawn after John Shearman, *Raphael's Cartoons in the Collection of Her Majesty the Queen and the Tapestries for the Sistine Chapel* (London, 1972).

FIG. 4. Raphael (1483–1520), *Mass at Bolsena*, 1512, fresco. Stanza d'Eliodoro, Vatican Apartments, Rome.

The processional carpet motif ended at the marble choir screen (originally set nearer the center of the chapel; again see cat. no. 17). Sixtus marked the choir screen with a pair of his own coat of arms—a vivid indication of how public and private coexisted in the chapel. The screen abutted a choir loft on the right wall, two-thirds of which opened to the entrance end of the chapel. The other third opened to the more prestigious altar end, reserved for the pope, cardinals, members of the papal bureaucracy, and prestigious lay and religious guests. Michelangelo later eloquently mirrored this division in his ceiling frescoes, reserving images of fallen mankind for the entrance end and biblical episodes containing God the Father for the altar zone.

Inside the choir screen, the processional path moved toward the high altar across a large pattern of nesting squares and circles. The twenty or so cardinals who sat on wooden benches around three of the sides of this so-called *quadratura* rose four different times during the mass to gather in a circle around its center. Other prelates sat on benches at the side of the chapel, while papal secretaries and others sat on the floor and on three steps facing the papal throne in front of the altar in the area known as the *vestibulum*, which also sometimes contained a movable pulpit. The pope's throne projected into the *vestibulum* from the left wall and stood at the same level as the *presbyterium*, which surrounded the altar. Once again, patterns inlaid on the floor instructed the celebrant where to stand during different parts of the mass. This was a carefully orchestrated and choreographed space. Raphael evocatively but idealistically recalls its component parts in his *Mass at Bolsena* fresco for the Vatican apartments (fig. 4). The differentiated garb of Swiss guards, cardinals, pope, acolytes, and onlookers, as well as the general splendor of the setting, all contributed to the effect of papal majesty.

SIXTUS'S DECORATIVE PROGRAM

In Sixtus's chapel, dedicated to the Assumption of the Virgin, all eyes would have been drawn to Perugino's large frescoed altarpiece on the altar wall. Sixtus purposefully chose the subject to honor the Virgin and lend visual support to the doctrine of Mary's Immaculate Conception, which he and his fellow Franciscans controversially claimed was confirmed by her bodily assumption into heaven. Sixtus also asked Perugino to paint scenes of the Finding of Moses and the Adoration of the Shepherds above it. Michelangelo destroyed all these works when he created his *Last Judgment*—a rare exception to his usual sensitivity to the work of his predecessors—but we can appreciate the general effect and iconography of the altarpiece from a workshop drawing (fig. 5). At the lower left Sixtus knelt in the company of the founders of the Roman Church. Saint Peter tapped the pope's shoulder with his keys, symbols of divine authority; Saint Paul, the famous apostle to the Gentiles, stood at the right. In the center, another kneeling figure directed the pope's gaze to the Virgin's appearance in heaven.

Sixtus's iconographic program began on the altar wall and continued along the sides of the chapel. Sitting on his throne, the pope looked directly at scenes from the life of Christ. Behind him appeared significant moments in the life of the great lawgiver Moses. Dichotomies and parallels dominated the organization of all of the chapel's decorations. In this case, Latin inscriptions above each pair of frescoes begin with similar wording and call attention to the pope's roles as priest, teacher, and ruler. The central fresco on the right wall in the entrance area of the chapel, Perugino's *Christ Giving the Keys to Saint Peter* (fig. 6), provides one of the clearest expositions of the theme of papal authority. Christ and the apostles

FIG. 5. Workshop of Perugino, *Copy of the Assumption Altarpiece for the Sistine Chapel.* Albertina, Vienna.

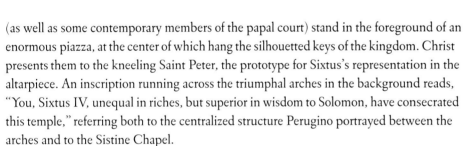

(as well as some contemporary members of the papal court) stand in the foreground of an enormous piazza, at the center of which hang the silhouetted keys of the kingdom. Christ presents them to the kneeling Saint Peter, the prototype for Sixtus's representation in the altarpiece. An inscription running across the triumphal arches in the background reads, "You, Sixtus IV, unequal in riches, but superior in wisdom to Solomon, have consecrated this temple," referring both to the centralized structure Perugino portrayed between the arches and to the Sistine Chapel.

Curiously, the main inscription over the entire scene offers a much less confident message than the foreground image and was probably intended for a sophisticated viewer, not a casual visitor. It reads: "Challenge to Jesus Christ, bearer of the law," which refers to a small scene in the left background of the fresco where Christ and his apostles pay a tax (the so-called tribute money). To interpret this scene, the viewer needed to look at the fresco opposite it with a similar label, "Challenge to Moses, bearer of the written law." There Sandro Botticelli showed Moses commanding the earth to open up and swallow four rebels, who were admonished in the inscription on a triumphal arch, "No one can assume the honor [of the priesthood] unless he is called by God, just as Aaron was." In other words, the papacy might be challenged, but it was always triumphant because its sources of power were uniquely legitimate.

Sixtus and his successors defended the papacy vigorously, whether in actual battles, paintings, or, as we have seen, the fortified architecture of the chapel itself. They boasted a glorious lineage through Christ himself, Saint Peter, and their predecessor popes. To bring this message home, Sixtus had the walls between the chapel's windows frescoed with a series of pre-Constantinian popes standing in niches. Christ, Saint Peter, and Paul probably stood in similar niches above the altarpiece. Even before imperial recognition by Constantine, the Church boasted strong and divinely sanctioned leaders.

FIG. 6. Pietro Perugino (1448–1523), *Christ Giving the Keys to Saint Peter*, 1481–82, fresco. Sistine Chapel.

The Ceiling

Adding frescoes to the extraordinarily complex and tightly organized decorative program was no easy matter. Sixtus left an unmistakably personal and institutional imprint on the chapel, including countless coats of arms that ran down the folds of the fictive silver and gold tapestries on the lowest zones of the wall. It would have seemed that little needed or could be added to his scheme, but with the passage of time and the election of his nephew as Pope Julius II, renovations became both necessary and desirable. The intertwined oak branches and bunches of acorns featured on the family's coats of arms now migrated to the ceiling, too, along with a staggering elaboration of the iconographic and decorative scheme.

The original decoration of the ceiling seems to have consisted of a deep blue ground studded with gold stars (see cat. no. 17). Julius initially thought of adding the twelve apostles, the first leaders of the Christian Church, to the portions of the vault between the chapel's windows. Michelangelo reportedly declared Julius's scheme a "poor thing," but he began sketching possibilities. One of his drawings (fig. 7) shows an enthroned figure surrounded by fashionable square and round geometric frames. Soon, however, Julius's imperial ambitions prevailed. It was he, after all, who had the hubris to command Donato Bramante to tear down the Constantinian basilica of old Saint Peter's and replace it with a new monumental, domed structure. For his part, Michelangelo had already imagined vast amounts of framing architecture, statues, and relief sculpture for Julius's tomb which could serve as the creative scaffolding for an unprecedentedly complex ceiling cycle. Julius's papal ambitions and Michelangelo's artistic ones aligned perfectly.

With the expansion of the program Michelangelo was able to create an extraordinary prequel to Sixtus's Moses and Christ cycles (figs. 8 and 9). The artist later claimed to have designed the ceiling completely on his own, but he probably received advice and counsel from the pope and court theologians, perhaps including the famed Augustinian preacher

FIG. 7. Michelangelo, *Initial Sketch for the Sistine Ceiling*, 1508, pen and ink. British Museum, London.

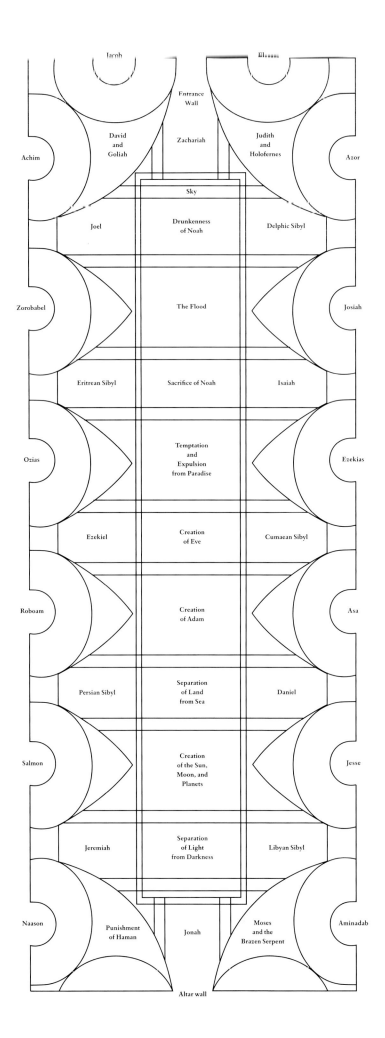

Jacob

Eleazar

Entrance
Wall

David
and
Goliah

Zachariah

Judith
and
Holofernes

Achim

Azor

Sky

Joel

Drunkenness
of Noah

Delphic Sibyl

Zorobabel

The Flood

Josiah

Eritrean Sibyl

Sacrifice of Noah

Isaiah

Ozias

Temptation
and
Expulsion
from Paradise

Ezekias

Ezekiel

Creation
of Eve

Cumaean Sibyl

Roboam

Creation
of Adam

Asa

Persian Sibyl

Separation
of Land
from Sea

Daniel

Salmon

Creation
of the Sun,
Moon, and
Planets

Jesse

Jeremiah

Separation
of Light
from Darkness

Libyan Sibyl

Naason

Punishment
of Haman

Jonah

Moses
and the
Brazen Serpent

Aminadab

Altar wall

FIG. 8 Plan of the Sistine ceiling. Redrawn after James S. Ackerman, *The Architecture of Michelangelo* (New York, 1961).

74

FIG. 9. The Sistine ceiling.

Egidio da Viterbo. Like the wall frescoes, the basic subject matter is easy to identify, though the subtle ways in which it is organized and presented allow for complex interpretation.

Michelangelo created a coherent architectural framing for the entire ceiling, effectively masking the vault's irregular curvature and the fact that the chapel is some three feet wider at the entrance than at the altar end. Nine openings—five small and four large—occupy the central spine of the vault. They contain key episodes from the creation of the world, the creation of humans, the fall of man, and stories from the life of Noah. Narrow strips of sky peak out at either end.

While the biblical narratives are designed to be seen while walking from the entrance of the chapel toward the altar, the rest of the ceiling is oriented toward the side walls. Michelangelo spent a good deal of creative energy devising pairs of idealized, twisting male nudes to provide the transition at either side of the smaller narratives (see cat. nos. 19, 20, and 23). He positioned them to either side of large bronze medallions depicting obscure Old Testament stories, principally taken from the Book of Maccabees.

The nudes perch on short pedestals that rise from projecting cornices and piers. Michelangelo aligned them with the outer edges of the preexisting frescoes of niches containing popes. Immediately below the nudes, pairs of putti frame large stone thrones on which sit ten prophets and sibyls, alternating by gender down the length of the chapel as well as across it. Two additional prophets sit at the short ends of the composition between scenes in the corner pendentives: *David and Goliath* and *Judith and Holofernes* at the entrance end; *Moses and the Brazen Serpent* and the *Punishment of Haman* over the altar. Pairs of tightly confined bronze nudes occupy the shadowy recesses between each throne. Finally, Michelangelo set groups of Christ's ancestors in the lunettes over the windows and in the triangular spandrels above them.

Designing, let alone executing, such a scheme offered unique challenges. Michelangelo hired at least a dozen collaborators to assist him with the preparation of the vault and his materials, as well as perhaps for realizing some of the repetitive architectural framing, putti, inscriptions, oak garlands, and the bronze medallions, whose compositions were lifted nearly directly from woodcuts in an early printed Bible. Michelangelo was no solitary artist. He knew nearly all his assistants beforehand, and most continued to work for him after the Sistine project was completed.

Michelangelo did not paint the chapel lying on his back, as is often asserted. Rather, he stood on a bridgelike platform. His good friend and advocate Giuliano da Sangallo may have advised him on its design and construction. Still, this was not easy work. Michelangelo and his assistants had to haul full-scale preparatory drawings, paints, and plaster up more than fifty feet in the air (the chapel is nearly sixty-eight feet tall), and Michelangelo worked so long with his head held back that he rightly complained in a self-deprecating sonnet in the Casa Buonarroti (fig. 10) that he had "grown a goiter like the cats of Lombardy." He also had difficulty focusing his eyes for a long time after completing the commission. On the Casa Buonarroti sheet we see him standing on the steps of his scaffolding next to the ironic words, "I am not in a good position and I am not a painter." Indeed, in 1508 Michelangelo had signed the contract for the ceiling as "Michelangelo, sculptor," but by the time he completed the work in 1512 he had proven himself a consummate painter too.

INTERPRETATION

That there is no single key to unraveling the meaning of Michelangelo's frescoes is not surprising given the range of visitors to the chapel and the vast intellectual resources brought to its interpretation by certain members of the papal court. This much is clear: the central narratives are arranged in reverse chronology, beginning over the entrance with the *Drunkenness of Noah* and moving back in time toward the first moments of creation over the altar. Thus, movement through the chapel and participation in its liturgies, not to mention loyalty to the

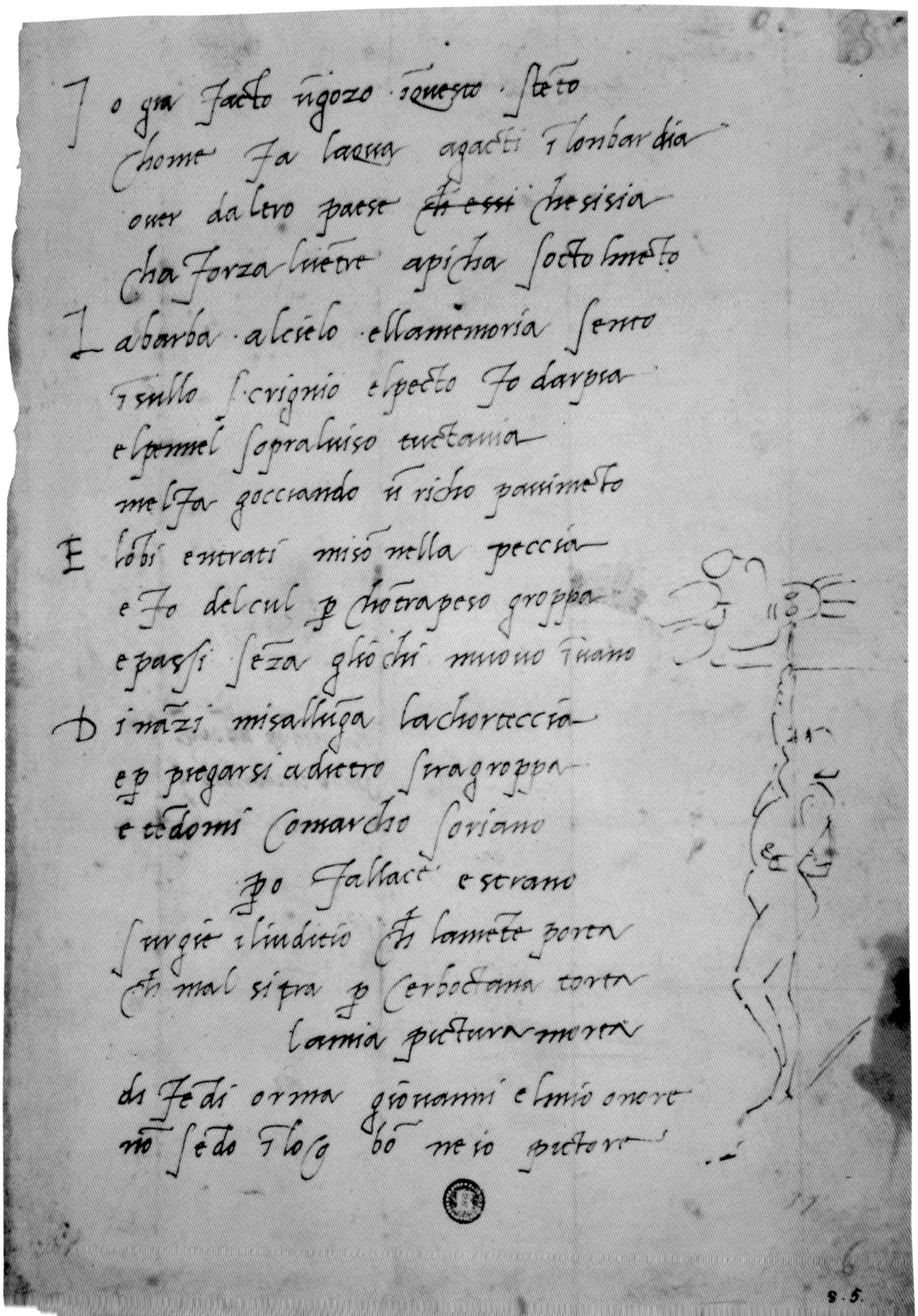

FIG. 10. Michelangelo, *Sonnet on Painting the Sistine Ceiling*, Archivio Buonarroti, XIII, f. iii.

FIG. 11. Michelangelo, *The Prophet Daniel, Cumaean Sibyl, and Nudes,* Sistine Chapel.

78

authority of the Church and its leader the pope, need to be understood as bringing humanity back into harmony with the divine. While the first scenes of the ceiling all deal with human sinfulness, as soon as one passes through the choir screen into the liturgically active second half of the chapel, Michelangelo shows God the Father physically present and interacting with his creation. Significantly, Michelangelo marked the juncture with the *Creation of Eve*, the Christian emblem of the Church and the antetype of the Virgin Mary, to whom the chapel is dedicated. Oneness with God replaces sinful separation from the divine as soon as one crosses over the threshold into the altar end of the chapel.

Michelangelo emphasized other dichotomous relationships in his representations of the prophets and sibyls, much as the earlier artists called attention to the parallels between Moses and Christ on the side walls. Pagan female sibyls alternate with Hebrew male prophets, all pointing to the same truths of salvation (fig. 11). Contrasts are evident, too, in age and pose. Innocent putti dance joyfully to either side of the seers' thrones, clearly participating in the light that comes from divine revelation. The bronze nudes in the shadows, on the other hand, struggle against revelation, turning inward, blindly butting their heads. Whether Michelangelo and his advisers were thinking about the contrast between Saint Augustine's City of God and the City of the World, as some art historical interpreters have suggested, or other dualistic schemes, it is clear that comparisons and contrasts abound.

Michelangelo painted the ancestors of Christ last and very quickly—some lunettes in as few as three days. He imagined them patiently but often lethargically awaiting the coming of salvation. Their attitudes may in part reflect Michelangelo's own personal exhaustion at the end of this enormous undertaking, but they also provide a powerful foil to the energized enthroned figures above and to the alert standing popes beneath them. In the case of Aminadab, Michelangelo clearly marked his figure as Jewish. Aminadab sports an earring and wears the yellow badge on his shoulder that all Jews in Rome were forced to display. Michelangelo offers a troubling if sympathetic portrait of an outsider in a Christian world.

Raphael's Tapestries

When Michelangelo completed his ceiling frescoes, every surface of the chapel was covered with figural decoration, save the lowest area of the side walls. Sixtus and his successors sometimes hung floral tapestries over the fictive gold and silver ones that had been painted there, but when Giovanni de' Medici was elected Pope Leo X (1513–21), he decided to commission narrative designs from Raphael. He must have sensed an opportunity to complete the apostolic component of the iconographic program, which had been abandoned when Julius's proposed apostle frescoes transmogrified into Michelangelo's prophets, sibyls, and Old Testament scenes. Leo also may have wanted to add a Medicean dimension to the insistent Della Rovere iconography in the chapel, effectively overlaying his personal commission on top of Sixtus's. Leo had his own coats of arms woven into the tapestry frames, and scenes from his life run along the lower borders.

Once again, a parallel cycle was planned: scenes from the life of Saint Paul on the left, the life of Peter on the right (see fig. 3). The program was largely restricted to the altar end of the chapel, though one tapestry, showing Saint Paul preaching at Athens, was to hang outside the choir screen. Tapestry was the ultimate luxury medium, and its expense as well as prestigiousness encouraged its concentration around the altar end of the chapel. As was his habit, Raphael worked quickly and fluently, producing ten full-size cartoons in gouache from 1515 to 1517. The tapestries, woven in Brussels by Pieter van Aelst, were all delivered to the Vatican before Leo's death in 1521. The cycle devoted to Saint Peter began with *The Miraculous Draft of Fishes* (fig. 12), capturing the dramatic moment when, after spending a futile night fishing, Peter, his brother Andrew, and their fellow fishermen are overwhelmed by an enormous catch. They immediately recognize Christ's hand in the miracle and pledge to become his apostles, "fishers of men." Raphael learned to make his figures large, muscular,

FIG. 12. Pieter van Aelst (1502–1550), after Raphael, *The Miraculous Draft of Fishes*, 1516–19, tapestry. Vatican Museums, Rome.

FIG. 13. Raphael (1483–1520), *Cartoon for Healing of the Lame Man*, 1515–16, gouache on paper. Victoria and Albert Museum, London.

and energetic from the example of the ceiling, where Michelangelo had begun painting relatively small figures but steadily increased their size and scale. Raphael also must have taken into account the numerous landscapes that unified the fifteenth-century frescoes on the side walls, lovingly describing reflections in the water, cranes and plants at the seashore, birds in flight, and a soft landscape in the distance. Never before had tapestry so successfully replicated the effects of painting, a testament both to the weaver's art and to Raphael, who overcame the additional challenge of having to draw his composition in reverse to accommodate the manufacturing process.

Raphael's cartoon for the *Healing of the Lame Man* (fig. 13), the tapestry of which was to hang directly under the fifteenth-century fresco of *Healing of the Leper* (see fig. 3), shows that Raphael assumed (correctly) that the weavers could replicate all the complexities he could imagine. Gold and silver threads allowed Van Aelst and his workshop to add luster to the twisting bronze columns with which Raphael filled the temple. Oil lamps glow in the distance. Raphael also arranged Peter and the lame man so that when the weaving reversed them, their position parallels the relation of Christ to the leper in the fresco above. Raphael's porphyry-colored frames around the tapestries also recalled the fresco frames. The chapel's decoration was complete and fully unified.

The Last Judgment

An act of vandalism—the tapestries were stolen during the Sack of Rome in 1527—contributed to one final and, in this case, disruptive intervention in the chapel. In 1533 Michelangelo began discussing a new altar wall program with Clement VII (1523–34), the second Medici pope and Leo X's cousin. Private, familial forces were once again at work in the chapel. Clement's initial idea seems to have been for a Resurrection, though some sources also talk about a Fall of the Rebel Angels for the entrance wall, both of which would have provided fitting visual retorts to the extreme humiliation that the pope and the entire Church had suffered during the Sack of Rome and the expanding Protestant Reformation. As it was, Clement died before Michelangelo set to painting, so the artist thought he would be able to return to the much delayed, unfinished tomb of Julius II. The new pope, Paul III Farnese (1534–49), however, had long hoped to have Michelangelo work for him and his family. Together Michelangelo and the pope agreed upon an enormous representation of the Last Judgment (fig. 14 and cat. nos. 26–29), a most fitting iconographical conclusion to decorations that already stretched from the beginning of time on the ceiling through the Gospels and the Acts of the Apostles (if we include the tapestries, which were eventually returned to the Vatican). The entire decorative scheme would now conclude with the final book of the Bible, Revelations.

Michelangelo initially hoped to save Perugino's altarpiece, as documented in an early sketch (cat. no. 26), but the subject matter called out for a scene of annihilation, and Michelangelo took the idea literally, destroying all the previous works on the altar wall. Unlike the rest of the decorations in the chapel, Michelangelo's *Last Judgment* includes no architectural framing; the end wall of the chapel seems literally blasted away. We know that the artist wanted the effect to be especially powerful, for he spent considerable time refacing the wall and thickening it at the top—not the bottom as one would expect—so that the entire scene observably tips into the space. At the same time Michelangelo paid homage to the earlier decorative scheme by dividing his composition into four levels that correspond to the pre existing divisions of the chapel walls (see fig. 1). In the lunettes at the top, at the height of Christ's ancestors, he placed angelic figures displaying the emblems of the Passion. Across the zone corresponding to the rows of pre-Constantinian popes, Michelangelo placed the Judging Christ and Virgin Mary surrounded by apostles, saints, and the elect in heaven, apt companions for the popes. Following the break marked by the cornice that runs under the windows, he showed souls rising to heaven and being dragged to hell as trumpeting angels

FIG. 14. Michelangelo, *Last Judgment*, 1536–41, fresco. Sistine Chapel.

in the center announce their fate. Finally, the top of the tapestry zone established the ground line of the landscape from which the dead arise and the condemned are driven across the River Styx to Hades.

When the fresco was unveiled in 1541 on the Feast of All Saints, it created an instant sensation. The pope is said to have fallen to his knees in awe, and art lovers were stupefied by the enormous amount of foreshortening, figural variety, and expression. But more than a few Church leaders raised their eyebrows. Michelangelo's brand of bold nudity increasingly was being rejected as inappropriate for religious works in the Counter-Reformation era; Michelangelo's Virgin was criticized for being shown inactive rather than as an advocate; and there was concern that without wings, angels could not be distinguished from saints.

Such reactions to the fresco resulted in the repainting of several figures and the addition of loincloths to numerous others (for greater detail of these revisions, see cat. no. 28). Here it may be worthwhile to call attention to those portions of the fresco that most affected how it was read. First, the character and meaning of Christ's and the Virgin's poses have been subjected to considerable debate. Following traditional descriptions of the end of time, Vasari and other early writers claimed that Christ was angry and vengeful, the Virgin quaking in his wake. But Michelangelo's Christ is young and Apollonian, and shows no ire. He raises his right arm in judgment, but he holds his left elegantly, even tenderly. Similarly, the Virgin seems to snuggle more than to cower. This composition may be unusually optimistic or at least more merciful than is generally recognized. Michelangelo shows vastly more saved souls than damned, including large numbers of women, not just men. To be sure, the trumpeting angels in the lower center of the composition hold a larger book toward the damned than the saved, but Michelangelo lavishes an extraordinarily large amount of wall space on the heavenly realm. The message would seem to be cautionary but hopeful.

Michelangelo's own features have been recognized on the flayed skin of Saint Bartholomew, who at the center of the fresco perilously dangles over sinners being dragged to hell. But this does place Michelangelo in the heavenly realm, after all, not among the condemned, suggesting a bit of black humor among the dread seriousness of the scene. Who but Michelangelo would also have dared portray Minos, standing at the entrance of hell, with the features of the papal master of ceremonies? And who but a knowledgeable, tolerant, and savvy patron like Paul III would have brushed away the request to have it changed, ironically opining that the pope held authority in heaven but not hell?

The decorative scheme of the Sistine Chapel, then, ended as it began, with Michelangelo contrasting good and evil, heaven and hell, openly acknowledging challenges, yet making it clear that virtue will triumph in the end. It was a very personal painting yet entirely accessible for public consumption and appreciation. It must have come as a bitter shock to Michelangelo that his Last Judgment engendered such controversy and negative reaction, leading soon after his death to censure and emendation. The Renaissance had come to an end, and public and private were no longer supposed to diverge or contrast. The willingness to entertain and consider dichotomies, to admit difficulties, and to appreciate multiple interpretive possibilities paled in the face of the dogmatic and authoritarian Counter-Reformation. Still, the chapel's decoration—pre- and post-Michelangelo, public and private—was destined to stand the test of time better than most any other Renaissance ensemble. Five centuries after its creation, the Sistine Chapel remains an extraordinarily beautiful and meaningful setting for papal masses and conclaves while also delighting and intriguing millions of visitors from the entire world.

17

G. TOGNETTI

The Sistine Chapel before the Interventions of Michelangelo (reconstruction)
1899
lithograph, 13 × 18⅛ in. (33.1 × 46.1 cm)
Biblioteca della Casa Buonarroti, B.1475.3.G.F.

The earliest-discovered reference to the Sistine Chapel dates to 1477. It can be traced to a poem dedicated to Pope Sixtus IV by the English humanist Robert Fleming, who celebrated the construction of the new chapel with these words: "pulchrum praestansque sacellum" (beautiful and excellent shrine). The plans of the aged yet still energetic Sixtus IV had called for the creation of a new chapel inside the structure built by Pope Nicholas III in 1278 and referred to as the "Magna Cappella Sacri Palatii" (Great Chapel of the Holy Palace). Although the building appeared grandiose and comparable to monuments from the imperial era, even on the outside, Sixtus IV focused mainly on the interior, wanting to make the chapel truly worthy of the presence of the pope during liturgical celebrations and rendering immediately evident the concept of "maiestas papalis" (papal majesty).

Tognetti's lithograph, an idealized reconstruction of what Sixtus IV intended, presents the chapel as it could be seen until the spring of 1504, when the vaulted ceiling with the starry sky was irreparably damaged by the opening of a wide crack. The lithograph, from which other later "ideal" views pertaining to successive historical stages of the chapel were derived, was published for the first time in the volume of illustrations included in Ernst Steinmann's monumental work of 1901–5. It may have been Steinmann himself who commissioned it from Tognetti; the print is signed and dated "Rome 1899." The artist, who might have been Gustavo Tognetti, an architect by trade and a professor at the University of Rome, is otherwise unknown.

Ettore Camesasca (1965) notes several discrepancies between Tognetti's reconstruction and the famous drawing by Piermatteo d'Amelia in the Uffizi depicting the chapel's vaulted ceiling. First, in the area above the altar, the space between the two vaults should not have had the appearance of a starry sky but should have been limited by a wide cornice. Second, according to the Uffizi drawing, the vaults should have been curved, as they otherwise appear, even in the first of Michelangelo's designs for the ceiling (preserved today among the drawings in the British Museum and the Detroit Institute of Arts). Finally, Tognetti altogether ignored the decoration between the corbels of the vaults.

These discrepancies notwithstanding, Tognetti's reconstruction remains an essential point of departure for studying the Sistine Chapel. First and foremost, it permits one to appreciate

BIBLIOGRAPHY

Aurelio Brandolini, *De Laudibus Sixti IV*, in Eugène Müntz, *Les arts à la cour des papes pendant le XVe et le XVIe siècle* (Paris, 1878–82), 3:56–60; Ernst Steinmann, *Die Sixtinische Kapelle* (Munich, 1901–5), 1:190–95; Ettore Camesasca, *Appendice*, in Roberto Salvini, *La Cappella Sistina in Vaticano* (Milan, 1965), 1:123–27, 152–53; John Shearman, *La costruzione della cappella e la prima decorazione al tempo di Sisto IV*, in *La Cappella Sistina. I primi restauri, la scoperta del colore* (Novara, 1986), 22–87; idem, *La storia della Cappella Sistina*, in *Michelangelo e la Sistina: la tecnica, il restauro, il mito*, exh. cat. (Rome, 1990), 19–29; Elena Lombardi, in *Vita di Michelangelo*, exh. cat., ed. Lucilla Bardeschi Ciulich and Pina Ragionieri (Florence, 2002), 48–49, no. 19.

at a glance the stylistic uniformity of the entire decorative plan that Sixtus IV desired, from the walls to the floor and the ceiling. Indeed, the original decoration possessed a profound unity, which Michelangelo's project disrupted. If the guidelines that Perugino established during the design phase of the decoration had been respected in the cycle of frescoes, the entire decorative system of the chapel would have found its place in a bright room, in which the walls were clearly and evenly marked out by frames and pilasters; the marble mosaic floor, inspired by medieval examples, defined and delimited the processional pathway leading up to the choir screen; the low barrel-vaulted ceiling connected to the walls by vaults and pendentives; and the whole chamber illuminated by six large windows on the side walls and by two more that opened on the wall above the altar. The large starry sky enclosed the vault according to the traditional model that extended from Early Christian mosaics to Giotto's Scrovegni Chapel. And for those who, like Redig de Campos (Salmi 1965), thought that the vastness of the ceiling dismayed the fifteenth-century painters, who, not daring to lay their hands on it, painted it blue and sprinkled it with golden stars," it is enough to remember the opening of Aurelio Brandolini's unconfirmed poem to show that contemporaries were more than happy with it: "Here is where the stars rise up to the heavenly temple . . ."

E.L.

18

ARTIST OF THE 19TH CENTURY

Vault of the Sistine Chapel (after Michelangelo)
before 1865
chromolithograph, 18⅛ × 40½ in. (46 × 103 cm),
    embedded on the surface of a table, made in Tuscany,
    from the same period, 25½ × 48 × 33⅛ in. (64 × 122 × 84 cm)
inv. 619

The many nineteenth-century artifacts preserved in Casa Buonarroti assume particular importance if one considers them as clues to the cultivation of the myth of Michelangelo in that
century, especially in the years following the celebration of the fourth centenary of his birth
(1875), when his masterpieces were reproduced using the most varied techniques. Among such
objects, the table shown here is undoubtedly among the most unusual. The chinoiserie decoration of its pedestal serves to make it a kind of "English-style" piece of furniture (although it was
made in Tuscany) completely in tune with the tastes of the period. In the Casa Buonarroti there
is a twin of this table that belonged to the last Buonarroti, Cosimo. In the indispensable *Guida
della Galleria Buonarroti* published in 1865, six years after the house became a corporate entity,
the piece is described by the first director of the museum, Angiolo Fabbrichesi: "a table with a
columnar pedestal, upon which there is a modern colored print reproduction of the paintings
on the ceiling of the Sistine Chapel." The two identical prints are not listed in the inventory
compiled by Alida Moltedo in 1991 of images that reproduce the Sistine Chapel. According to
Tolnay (1972), they are "the first chromolithographs of the ceiling, made by the German artist
Ludwig Grüner in London around 1830."

P.R.

BIBLIOGRAPHY

Angiolo Fabbrichesi, *Guida
della Galleria Buonarroti*
(Florence, 1865), 22; Charles
de Tolnay, *L'omaggio a
Michelangelo di Albrecht
Dürer* (Rome, 1972), 14;
Alida Moltedo, *La Sistina
riprodotta*, exh. cat. (Rome,
1991).

MICHELANGELO

Study of Two Nudes for the Sistine Ceiling
1509–10
black chalk and black charcoal on paper, 12¼ × 8⅜ in. (30.1 × 21.3 cm)
inv. 33 F

The drawing includes two studies, each very different, for two figures on the ceiling of the Sistine Chapel. On top is a nude seated on a cubical block, which Steinmann in 1905 connected to the Ignudo located to the left above the prophet Daniel. In the fresco, however, the posture of the arm and the torsion of the head are different. Finding a comparative reference for the sketch on the bottom proves more difficult. It is executed with schematic strokes that seem to recall the beginnings of Michelangelo's thinking for the ceiling. Michael Hirst (personal communication) has conjectured, in fact, that it should be linked to the design for two female figures in the lunettes with the Ancestors of Christ.

While Berenson (1938) offhandedly dismissed the drawing, claiming that he was not able to "decide whether this kind of scribbling could be by Michelangelo," more considered opinions on the question are not lacking. Wilde (1953) finds convincing parallels between this sheet and one by Michelangelo in the British Museum (inv. 1859-6-25-5589), both of which he firmly believes to be original autograph works and connected by penetrating technical and stylistic similarities. Paola Barocchi (1962) discerns in the drawing one of the moments in which "the artist sketches out the poetic idea with a lively flourish, without determining it, but rather implying in the ruffled marking a multitude of possible solutions."

The highly emotional style of Michelangelo apparent in the upper figure persuaded the curators of the exhibition "Rodin and Michelangelo" to include it in their comparison of the two artists, notwithstanding that evidence of the drawing's circulation during the nineteenth century is nonexistent, as Flavio Fergonzi (1996) points out.

P.R.

BIBLIOGRAPHY

Ernst Steinmann, *Die Six-tinische Kapelle* (Munich, 1901–5), 595, no. 14; Bernard Berenson, *The Drawings of Florentine Painters* (Chicago and London, 1938), 2:227, no. 661c; Johannes Wilde, *Italian Drawings in the Department of Prints and Drawings in the British Museum: Michelangelo and His Studio* (London, 1953), 21, no. 9; Paola Barocchi, *Michelangelo e la sua scuola. I disegni di Casa Buonarroti e degli Uffizi* (Florence, 1962), 1:27, no. 17; idem, *Michel-angelo. Mostra di disegni, manoscritti e documenti*, exh. cat. (Florence, 1964), 13–14, no. 23; Charles de Tolnay, *Corpus dei disegni di Michel-angelo* (Novara, 1975–80), 1:31, no. 24; Flavio Fergonzi, in *Michelangelo nell'Otto-cento. Rodin e Michelangelo*, exh. cat., ed. Maria Mimita Lamberti and Christopher Riopelle (Milan, 1996), 148–51, no. 33; Pina Ragionieri, in *Images of Salvation: Master-pieces from Vatican and Italian Collections*, exh. cat., ed. Giovanni Morello (Rome, 2002), 111, no. 19.

Michelangelo, *Nude Above and to the Left of the Prophet Daniel*, Sistine Chapel.

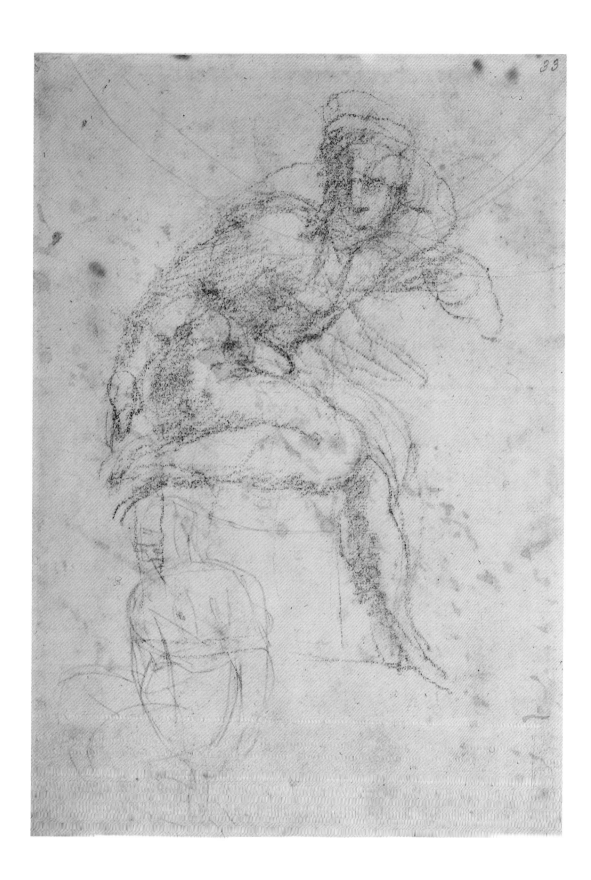

MICHELANGELO

Study of a Nude for the Sistine Ceiling
1508–9
black chalk on paper, 4½ × 2⅝ in. (11.4 × 6.6 cm)
inv. 49 F

This small drawing, which has been cut out and reinforced, most likely was trimmed down from a larger sheet after the completeness of its content had been recognized. Careless actions of this kind are anything but rare in the complex fortunes of older graphic works; they constitute a difficult part of their history. Nonetheless, the vigorous and compact little figure in the center of the sheet has for a long time been considered autograph by the most authoritative Michelangelo scholars, who also agree in connecting the drawing with two nude figures on the ceiling of the Sistine Chapel, namely the one above and to the right of the prophet Isaiah (regarding the upper part of the sketch) and the one to the left of the Cumaean Sibyl, on account of the position of the legs. The sheet is dated, in fact, on the basis of the identification with the nudes on the ceiling, as it appears to represent a preparatory phase of their composition. It is worth underscoring that only a few dozen sketches survive from Michelangelo's huge undertaking for the Sistine ceiling, which no doubt included voluminous preparatory studies. But the artist habitually destroyed his own drawings, in keeping with his desire that no unfinished elements should remain from his projects.

Michelangelo's decoration of the Sistine ceiling took place in two phases. The first half of the work, up to and including the *Creation of Eve*, was completed between the summers of 1508 and 1510. The two nudes to which our drawing is related appear in this section. Michelangelo began by painting from the door of the chapel toward the altar so that liturgical celebrations could continue during the initial phase of the work. For this reason, the scenes painted first

BIBLIOGRAPHY

Paola Barocchi, *Michelangelo e la sua scuola. I disegni di Casa Buonarroti e degli Uffizi* (Florence, 1962), 26, no. 16; Michael Hirst, "I disegni preparatori," in *Michelangelo. La Cappella Sistina*, ed. Kathleen Weil-Garris Brandt (Novara, 1994), 3:73–76; Pina Ragionieri, *Miguel Angel entre Florencia y Roma*, exh. cat. (Valencia, 1997), 186–87, no. 37; Pina Ragionieri, *Michelangelo: The Man and the Myth*, exh. cat. (Syracuse, NY, 2008), 94, no. 16.

Michelangelo, *Nude Above and to the Left of the Cumaean Sibyl*, Sistine Chapel.

were iconographically the last; in other words, their execution started with the stories of Noah and went back to the Creation. The scaffolding for the second half of the ceiling was erected in the spring of 1511, and from there the work proceeded quickly until its completion in late October 1512. Within the continuous form of the painted architecture that supports the whole work, one witnesses a progressive increase in dramatic quality in this second phase, inasmuch as the figures become larger in size and the compositions appear ever more freely arranged. Meanwhile the use of gold, one of the last vestiges of the fifteenth-century workshops, is reduced to practically nothing.

P.R.

21

MICHELANGELO

Study of a Man's Face for the "Flood" on the Sistine Ceiling
1509–10
red chalk on paper, 4⅞ × 5⅝ in. (12.5 × 14.2 cm)
inv. 47 F

This drawing of a male face, by its intense and concentrated expression, may be presumed on stylistic grounds to be from the period of Michelangelo's work on the vaulted ceiling of the Sistine Chapel, even if, among the critics, there is a slight chronological back and forth between the years of the cartoon for the *Battle of Cascina* (1504–5) and preparations for the ceiling (1508–12). Two figures from the Sistine Chapel have credibly been compared to this sheet: the figure that supports a nude in the right-hand portion of the *Flood*, and the figure at the left of the same composition who is caught in the act of climbing a tree. In this evocative half-profile, Wilde has correctly discerned a realistic passion, rare for Michelangelo in this type of study. Indeed, the face is bent slightly forward and the eyelids lowered in a manner that makes it resemble a death mask.

P.R.

BIBLIOGRAPHY

Johannes Wilde, *Italian Drawings in the Department of Prints and Drawings in the British Museum: Michelangelo and His Studio* (London, 1953), 97; Paola Barocchi, *Michelangelo e la sua scuola. I disegni di Casa Buonarroti e degli Uffizi* (Florence, 1962), 1:33–34, no. 22; Charles de Tolnay, *Corpus dei disegni di Michelangelo* (Novara, 1975–80), 1:100–101, no. 24; Pina Ragionieri, *Michelangelo: Drawings and Other Treasures from the Casa Buonarroti, Florence*, exh. cat. (Atlanta, 2001), 130–31, no. 33.

Michelangelo, *Male Figure in a Tree*, detail of the *Flood*, Sistine Chapel.

22

MICHELANGELO

Study for an Arm on the Sistine Ceiling
1509–10
black chalk on paper, 3⅞ × 5⅛ in. (9.8 × 13.1 cm)
inv. 8 F

The technique that Michelangelo uses here of rather energetic marking, exalted by the plastic use of chiaroscuro, prompted Luciano Berti (1985) to define it (in this and other similar youthful works) as "drawing by sculpting." He sees in this drawing a probable memory of the ancient discus thrower but, above all, a powerful hand related to a motif explored in *David* and repeatedly present in the figures of the Sistine Chapel ceiling. It is not by chance that critics have ascribed this right forearm—extended horizontally and charged with vitality, in spite of its static position—to different figures: Frey (1909), for instance, sees it as the arm of God the Father in the *Creation of Adam*, while Wilde (1953) and Tolnay refer to it as the mirror opposite of the drunken Noah's left arm. They believed the drawing belonged to the much later period of the *Last Judgment*, but most scholars agree that it exhibits the salient characteristics of the young artist's style and spirituality during the time he was still sculpting *David* and beginning the Sistine project.

P.R.

BIBLIOGRAPHY

Karl Frey, *Die Handzeich-nungen Michelagniolos Buonarroti* (Berlin, 1909), 1:109–10, no. 232; Johannes Wilde, *Italian Drawings in the Department of Prints and Drawings in the British Museum: Michelangelo and His Studio* (London, 1953), 16; Paola Barocchi, *Michelangelo e la sue scuola. I disegni di Casa Buonarroti e degli Uffizi* (Florence, 1962), 31, no. 20; Charles de Tolnay, *Corpus dei disegni di Michelangelo* (Novara, 1975–80), 1:100, no. 122; Luciano Berti, *Michelangelo. I disegni di Casa Buonarroti* (Florence, 1985), 14; Pina Ragionieri, *Michelangelo: Drawings and Other Treasures from the Casa Buonarroti, Florence*, exh. cat. (Atlanta, 2001), 134–35, no. 35.

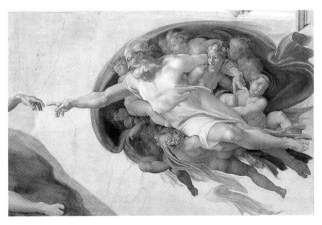

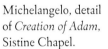

Michelangelo, detail of *Creation of Adam*, Sistine Chapel.

Michelangelo, *Drunkenness of Noah*, Sistine Chapel.

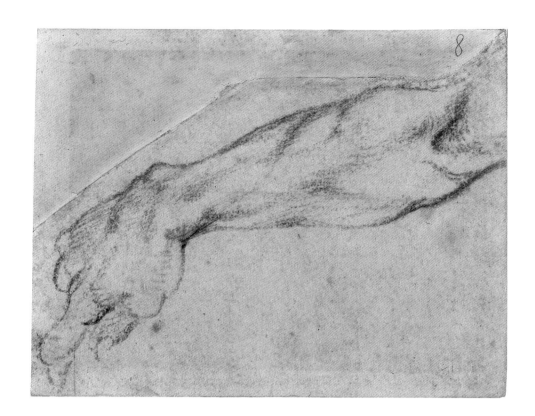

23

MICHELANGELO

Studies of Legs for the Sistine Ceiling
1508–9
black chalk on paper, 10¼ × 7¾ in. (26 × 19.6 cm)
inv. 52 F

Among Michelangelo's drawings at the Casa Buonarroti, this sheet belongs to a group of five studies of legs, four of which (10 F, 11 F, 44 F, 48 F) are attributable to the years in which the master was occupied with the complex construction of the New Sacristy in the church of San Lorenzo in Florence. They are regarded as unquestionably autograph in modern scholarly studies from Thode (1908–13) to Wilde (1953).

The fifth drawing in the series, shown here, relates instead to the preceding years, the period in which the artist worked in blissful solitude on the decoration of the Sistine Chapel ceiling. In the center, there is a left leg whose impact is undeniable: the foot is vigorously planted on the ground and the calf drawn with expressive finesse. At the beginning of the twentieth century, Steinmann had already recognized it as a study for the nude above and to the right of the Delphic Sibyl. Next to it, a right leg brushes the ground with just the tip of the foot. Thode was able to determine (once again, at the beginning of the twentieth century) that it represents a preparatory design for the nude above and to the right of the prophet Isaiah.

The autograph nature of this drawing has been affirmed by Wilde (1953), among others, but doubts have been expressed over the years by scholars such as Paola Barocchi (1962–64) and Charles de Tolnay (1975–80), due perhaps to the existence of many copies of anatomical studies of this kind made from sketches by important artists. Nevertheless, the drawing overall possesses a sureness of line that obliges one to see in it the hand of Michelangelo.

P.R.

BIBLIOGRAPHY

Henry Thode, *Michelangelo. Kritische Untersuchungen über seine Werke* (Berlin, 1908–13), 1:258, 3: no. 47; Johannes Wilde, *Italian Drawings in the Department of Prints and Drawings in the British Museum: Michelangelo and His Studio* (London, 1953), 19 ff; Paola Barocchi, *Michelangelo e la sua scuola. I disegni di Casa Buonarroti e degli Uffizi* (Florence, 1962–64), 1:276–77, no. 227; Charles de Tolnay, *Corpus dei disegni di Michelangelo* (Novara, 1975–80), 1:109–10, no. 142.

Michelangelo, *Studies of Legs*, Casa Buonarroti, inv. 10 F.

Michelangelo, *Nude Above and to the Right of the Delphic Sibyl*, Sistine Chapel.

Michelangelo, *Nude Above and to the Right of the Prophet Isaiah*, Sistine Chapel.

24

MICHELANGELO

Study for Adam in the "Expulsion from Paradise" on the Sistine Ceiling
1509–10
black chalk on paper, 10⅜ × 7½ in. (26.2 × 19.2 cm)
inv. 45 F

"A sketch, in black chalk, of a nude male figure, turned slightly to the right in a gesture of fear; the head and part of the legs are not drawn. An idea for Adam expelled from the earthly Paradise, painted in fresco on the ceiling of the Sistine Chapel in Rome." This is how, in 1875, Aurelio Gotti, director of the Regie Gallerie Fiorentine and a biographer of Michelangelo, described this sheet.

The well-crafted and certainly autograph drawing appeared to Paola Barocchi (1962) to be an expression of a very mature idea, executed with "almost greater" satisfaction than the corresponding figure painted on the ceiling. Indeed, comparison between this graphic study and the execution of the final version reveals obvious affinities. Nevertheless, as one would expect, some minor variations exist, which serve to legitimize Barocchi's opinion. Michael Hirst (1988) succeeds in effectively defining the rapid stroke of this drawing, which reveals Michelangelo's approach to capturing the plasticity of the human body once the basic idea of the figure had been established and the artist was conditioned by the movement he himself had chosen.

P.R.

BIBLIOGRAPHY

Aurelio Gotti, *Vita di Michelangelo Buonarroti narrata con l'aiuto di nuovi documenti* (Florence, 1875), 2:191; Paola Barocchi, *Michelangelo e la sua scuola. I disegni di Casa Buonarroti e degli Uffizi* (Florence, 1962), 28, no. 18; Michael Hirst, *Michelangelo and His Drawings* (New Haven and London, 1988), 27, 61; Pina Ragionieri, *Michelangelo: Drawings and Other Treasures from the Casa Buonarroti, Florence*, exh. cat. (Atlanta, 2001), 132–33, no. 34.

Michelangelo, *Expulsion from Paradise*, Sistine Chapel.

25

MICHELANGELO

Study for a Figure from the "Punishment of Haman" on the Sistine Ceiling
1511–12
red chalk on paper, 6¼ × 8⅝ in. (15.9 × 21.8 cm)
inv. 12 F

While the debate over the attribution of this drawing to Michelangelo is not yet over, its relationship to the *Punishment of Haman*, which occupies the central portion of one of the pendentives of the Sistine Chapel ceiling, is certain. In his representation of the scene, Michelangelo broke from the Old Testament tradition by depicting the subject not hanging from a gallows but crucified, with an assuredly dramatic emphasis on the justice of his punishment. The story of Haman is narrated in the Bible in the Book of Esther. As vizier for the Persian king Ahasuerus, Haman mounted a persecution of the Jews but was exposed and condemned, together with his sons and supporters. In the episode depicted on the ceiling, analogous to the scenes in the other pendentives (*Judith and Holofernes, David and Goliath, Moses and the Brazen Serpent*), Michelangelo portrays a difficult moment for the Jewish people that is happily overcome. The victory over the persecution of Haman is commemorated in the Jewish religious tradition by the feast of Purim, which is celebrated each year between February and March. For the occasion, it is still customary to prepare sweets that are called "Haman ears."

BIBLIOGRAPHY

Paola Barocchi, *Michelangelo e la sua scuola. I disegni di Casa Buonarroti e degli Uffizi* (Florence, 1962), 223–24, no. 176; Charles de Tolnay, *I disegni di Michelangelo nelle collezioni italiane*, exh. cat. (Florence, 1975), 34; Tessie Vecchi, in *Michelangelo e la Sistina. La tecnica, il restauro, il mito*, exh. cat. (Rome, 1991), 306, no. 198; Carmen Bambach, "Problemi di tecnica nei cartoni di Michelangelo per la Cappella Sistina," in *Michelangelo. La Cappella Sistina*, ed. Kathleen Weil-Garris Brandt (Novara 1994), 3:96–97; idem, *Drawing and Painting in the Italian Renaissance Workshop* (Cambridge, 1999), 279–81.

Michelangelo, detail of
Punishment of Haman,
Sistine Chapel.

The dating of the drawing is derived from the fact that Michelangelo executed this scene during the final phase of his work on the ceiling, that is, between 1511 and 1512. On the right, a pensive figure intently reads from a book. The relationship of this figure to one beside King Ahasuerus's bed in the ceiling pendentive is clear. The outstretched arm with the hand partially traced over in pen, in the middle of the sheet, corresponds to the right arm of the youth dressed in yellow, who, in the same episode, is coming down the stairs. It is worth noting that in the fresco the arm is covered by a robe, while in the drawing it is exposed. The hand in the lower left corner of the sheet is a repetition of the left hand of the reading figure discussed above.

The *Punishment of Haman* is the Sistine ceiling episode for which the greatest number of graphic works by Michelangelo survive. This fact acquires a rather interesting meaning if one keeps in mind the many original drawings that were lost, for the most part destroyed by the master, during his life and especially in his extreme old age. The mass of surviving studies in this case suggests how intensive Michelangelo's graphic preparation must have been.

P R

MICHELANGELO

Study for the "Last Judgment"
1533–34
black chalk on paper, reinforced with pen and ink at a later date,
16⅜ × 11¾ in. (41.5 × 29.8 cm)
inv. 65 F

In 1536, twenty-four years after the completion of the decoration of the Sistine ceiling, Michelangelo, then sixty-one years old, confronted the wall behind the chapel altar. He had been given the assignment three years earlier by Pope Clement VII; following Clement's death the project was confirmed in 1534 by his successor, Paul III. The important commission was one reason the artist left Florence, never to return.

The large wall was not completely empty, however. At first, the master tried to avoid destroying the existing decoration, in particular Perugino's *Assumption of the Virgin*, the subject to which the chapel was dedicated. This famous drawing bears witness to it: clearly visible, in the lower middle, is the framing of the fifteenth-century altarpiece around which the souls of the damned contort in discord. Yet from this same sheet, which provides the only surviving graphic evidence treating the whole wall, we can understand that the dynamic totality of the fresco was already clear in Michelangelo's mind, with Christ the Judge as the powerful motive force behind the entire action. From this sprang the necessity of abandoning hope of saving Perugino's altarpiece. Let us look at the result of this decision: in the gigantic scene, completely liberated and highlighted by the azure energy of the lapis-lazuli background, bodies float in the air with a slow and uninterrupted rotary motion by dint of their muscles, without the help of wings, which are absent even from the angels. The violations of traditional iconography in the *Last Judgment* are beyond number: one of the most obvious is the insertion of the boat of the mythological ferryman of souls, Charon—a patent reference to Dante.

When the work was unveiled on November 1, 1541, it caused great consternation and drew innumerable criticisms. These were directed predominantly at the iconographic anomalies and the sizable number of naked figures. The work risked total destruction, but the superhuman fame that Michelangelo had gained by that time limited the damage, as such, to the covering-up of some of the nudity and the obliteration and repainting of a few figures. This happened through the intervention of Daniele da Volterra, Michelangelo's student and close friend, who in this way contributed, perhaps willingly, to the rescue of the masterpiece.

P.R.

BIBLIOGRAPHY

Johannes Wilde, *Italian Drawings in the Department of Prints and Drawings in the British Museum: Michelangelo and His Studio* (London, 1953), 65, 90, 100; Paola Barocchi, *Michelangelo e la sua scuola. I disegni di Casa Buonarroti e degli Uffizi* (Florence, 1962), 1:177–79, no. 142; Charles de Tolnay, *Corpus dei disegni di Michelangelo* (Novara, 1975–80), 3:21–23, no. 347; Johannes Wilde, *Michelangelo: Six Lectures* (Oxford, 1978), 162.

ARTIST OF THE SECOND HALF OF THE 16TH CENTURY

Two Resurrected Figures (after the engraving by Nicholas Béatrizet of the *Last Judgment*)
after 1562
red chalk on blue paper, 9 × 9⅛ in. (22.8 × 23.2 cm)
inv. 20 F

This small sheet, like others that have been in the Casa Buonarroti drawings collection since the time of Michelangelo's direct descendants, was traditionally regarded as an original preparatory drawing by Buonarroti for the *Last Judgment* fresco (in modern times it was still considered as such by Delacre [1938]). Today, scholarly consensus maintains that it is a copy of modest quality that can be dated to the second half of the sixteenth century, as Paola Barocchi (1962) has proposed, on the basis of its academic character. The small scrap of blue paper—what remains of a sheet that was badly cut on all sides—portrays the half bust of a male figure leaning on his right elbow with his head and left arm raised, together with the head and shoulders of another figure, portrayed in profile and leaning forward. Given the measurements of the fragment, it is possible that the unknown copyist drew a more expansive scene on a sheet of large dimensions that was then cut down, isolating the group of heads, in a format that perhaps was meant to mimic the portion of a drawing corresponding to a *giornata* (a day's work in fresco) for purely commercial motives. Indeed, while Michelangelo was still alive, competition broke out to snap up his drawings—as several records attest, such as the letters of Pietro Aretino, who insistently begged the artist to make him a gift of some drawings. The competition only intensified after his death. One must consider, moreover, especially in the case of the *Last Judgment*, the explosive phenomenon of copies made using the most varied techniques, particularly engravings. The latter began proliferating as soon as the fresco was uncovered, their makers deaf to warnings of the presumed heterodoxy of the work. Many of these copies were "badly produced by the greed of the printmakers, who were motivated more by profit than by honor" (Vasari).

The fragment owned by Casa Buonarroti is derived from one of these poorly produced prints, one of a series of ten engravings by Nicolas Béatrizet that is dated 1562 (Bartsch, XV, 257, 37). By that time, calls for the destruction of the fresco or at least its modification were being heard. The drawing is a copy of part of the lower portion of the frescoed *Last Judgment* wall: the two figures, placed near Charon's boat and the mouth of Hell, seem to emerge from the bowels of the earth, their newly reacquired fleshly bodies heaving with tremendous labor and suffering.

The drawing is characterized by a certain harshness of line that somewhat uncertainly follows the outlines of the bodies, hesitating upon the most demanding details of the faces and the hand in the foreground, and by an accentuated chiaroscuro effect—qualities that demonstrate adherence to the style of Michelangelo. The choice of a colored support accentuates the "pictorial" character of the drawing in red chalk, which is used to render the voluminous spaces with light strokes and shading inside the contours, distorting the eminently plastic character of the model.

The direct derivation from Béatrizet's engraving is evidenced by the position of the left hand of the figure in the upper portion of the drawing. Here the hand is separated from the

BIBLIOGRAPHY

Henry Thode, *Michelangelo. Kritische Untersuchungen über seine Werke* (Berlin, 1908–13), 2:13, 3:81; Maurice Delacre, *Le dessin de Michel-Ange* (Brussels, 1938), 237; Luitpold Dussler, *Die Zeichnungen des Michelangelo. Kritische Katalog* (Berlin, 1959), 214, no. 419; Paola Barocchi, *Michelangelo e la sua scuola. I disegni di Casa Buonarroti e degli Uffizi* (Florence, 1962), 324–25, no. 284; Marcella Marongiu, in *Giovan Battista Moroni. Lo sguardo sulla realtà 1560–1579*, exh. cat., ed. S. Facchinetti (Milan, 2004), 240–41, no. 45.

face, while in the Sistine fresco and the earlier printed copies (Della Casa, Bonasone, Ghisi) the thumb brushes against the chin. Moreover, a larger portion of this figure's chest is shown because the resurrected figure in the foreground is depicted farther down. This figure betrays the dependence of the drawing on the print even in the features of the face, which are sharper, and by its pronounced traits, especially the profile of the nose and chin.

M.M.

28A–L

GIORGIO GHISI (MANTUA 1520–1582)

Last Judgment (after Michelangelo)
Late 1540s; edition of ten images printed between 1823 and 1870
engraving: a) *Lunette with Symbols of the Passion,* 9½ × 20½ in. (24 × 52 cm); b) *Lunette
   with Symbols of the Passion,* 17¼ × 17⅛ in. (43.7 × 43.5 cm); c) *Group of Martyrs and
   Saints,* 17¼ × 17⅛ in. (43.7 × 43.5 cm); d) *Christ the Judge, Virgin, and Saints,* 17⅜ × 19 in.
   (44 × 48.2 cm); e) *Group of the Blessed,* 15⅜ × 10¾ in. (39 × 27.4 cm); f) *Battle between
   Angels and the Damned,* 12½ × 15⅝ in. (31.7 × 39.8 cm); g) *Trumpeting Angels,* 13⅝ × 12¼ in.
   (34.6 × 31 cm); h) *The Blessed and Angels,* 14 × 20⅞ in. (35.5 × 53 cm); i) *Charon's Boat,*
   14 × 20⅞ in. (35.5 × 53 cm); l) *Group of Resurrected Souls,* 12¼ × 22½ in. (31 × 57 cm)
inv. 563

Among the large number of prints featuring Michelangelo's work published during the second
half of the sixteenth century—prints that were often mediocre and plentiful on account of the
greed of their publishers—Giorgio Vasari, in his life of Marcantonio Raimondi (1568), ranked
this *Last Judgment* by Ghisi among the few that should be saved. The work has indeed enjoyed
great fame over the intervening centuries, due in large part to the fact that when assembled
together, its ten plates (marked in Italian alphabetical sequence A through L) form a complete
reproduction of the Sistine fresco. That there are no less than nine editions of this rendering of
the *Last Judgment* confirms its prestige. So, too, does the fact that the original engraved plates
survive today in Rome, at the Istituto Nazionale per la Grafica, where they were moved from the
Calcografia Camerale, whose mark is stamped on the sheets belonging to the Casa Buonarroti.
They come from the edition reissued by the printer Giovanni Giacomo de' Rossi (1627–1691),
in which sheet I carries, below Charon's boat, a dedication to Mathys van de Merwede, lord
of Clootwyck and a patron of artists, who was in Italy between 1647 and 1650. This dedication
replaces the inscription in praise of Michelangelo that appears on older imprints. The Casa's
series of prints was made from the heavily retouched plates in 1823, when the nude figures were
covered with additional draperies and shadows.

   One notices here, as in other famous engravings by Ghisi, the refined engraving (*bulino*)
technique he first learned while studying drawing in Mantua with Giulio Romano. Ghisi then
received thorough instruction in Rome from Marcantonio Raimondi. In addition, while on a
sojourn in Antwerp, he fully appreciated the dictates of the Flemish school of engraving, which
devoted much attention to Michelangelo's models.

   Alida Moltedo (1991) describes well his mastery when she affirms that in this series "the
engraver strives to go beyond a mere iconographical record of the scene and to instead capture
its overall impression. Though divided into groups, it is at once nourished by a single dynamic
energy." Ghisi's project was recognized as one of the most extensive and complicated print-
making endeavors of its era and was abundantly copied, both as a set and as separate sheets,
from the time of its appearance. The most well-known copyist of Ghisi's *Last Judgment* was the
sixteenth-century French engraver Nicolas Béatrizet, who faithfully replicated the individual
lines while conferring a personal stamp upon his work, particularly in the facial features.

P.R.

BIBLIOGRAPHY

Alida Moltedo, *La Sistina
riprodotta,* exh. cat. (Rome,
1991), 68–72, no. 17; *Indice
delle stampe De' Rossi. Con-
tributo alla storia di una Stam-
peria romana,* ed. Anna Grelle
Iusco (Rome, 1996), 449;
Paolo Bellini, *L'opera incisa
di Giorgio Ghisi* (Bassano
del Grappa, 1998), 213–17;
Pina Ragionieri, *Michel-
angelo: Drawings and Other
Treasures from the Casa
Buonarroti, Florence,* exh.
cat. (Atlanta, 2001), 140–49,
nos. 38–47.

28 A *Lunette with Symbols of the Passion*

28 B *Lunette with Symbols of the Passion*

28C *Group of Martyrs and Saints*

28D *Christ the Judge, Virgin, and Saints*

28E *Group of the Blessed*

28F *Battle between Angels and the Damned*

28G *Trumpeting Angels*

28H *The Blessed and Angels*

29

CIRCLE OF GIULIO CLOVIO (GRIZANE 1498–ROME 1578)

Last Judgment (after Michelangelo)
c. 1570
tempera on parchment, 12⅝ × 9 in. (32 × 23 cm)
inv. Gallerie 1890, no. 810

This miniature came from the Medici collections at the Uffizi to the Casa Buonarroti in the 1930s. The parchment depicts the Sistine Chapel's *Last Judgment*, with all its 391 figures and without any of the famous additions of censorship to which the original had been subjected. Here all the original nudes can be seen, including the group that created the greatest scandal: Saint Blaise, with brushes in hand, who observes Saint Catherine on her wheel of martyrdom (on the far right, halfway up the composition). This group not only was "trousered" but was even completely repainted by Daniele da Volterra in 1565.

According to Giovanni Agosti (1989), this miniature recalls the engraving executed from the *Last Judgment* in 1569 by Dalmatian artist Martino Rota, however indirectly and referring to evidence that clearly predated 1565. The small variations are, however, significant: for instance, Christ is given back his beard, the absence of which in the fresco had been strongly criticized. At the top of the composition in the miniature version, where Rota in his engraving had set a portrait of Michelangelo, we see, in obedience to Counter-Reformation prescriptions, representations of God and the Holy Spirit. The work's stylistic characteristics ascribe it to Giulio Clovio, the most important miniaturist of the sixteenth century.

P.R.

BIBLIOGRAPHY

Giovanni Agosti, "Un Giudizio universale in miniatura," *Annali della Scuola Normale Superiore di Pisa*, ser. 3, 19, no. 4 (1989): 1291–97; Pina Ragionieri, *Michelangelo: Drawings and Other Treasures from the Casa Buonarroti*, Florence, exh. cat. (Atlanta, 2001), 138–39, no. 37.

30

FRANCESCO BARBAZZA (ACTIVE ROME, LATE 18TH CENTURY)

View of the Sistine Chapel (after a drawing by Francesco Panini [1738–1800])
1766
etching, 19⅛ × 27⅛ in. (48.5 × 69 cm)
inv. 54

The caption along the bottom can be translated: *Drawn by Francesco Panini.   VIEW   Engraved
by Francesco Barbazza / The Sistine Chapel in the Apostolic Vatican Palace, built by Pope Sixtus
IV under the direction of Baccio Pintelli [sic] Florentine Architect and decorated under Popes
Julius II, Clement VII and Paul III. / 1: Far right portion of the altar of the Chapel. 2: The papal
throne and, to the right, the seats for the Sacred College. 3: The choir screen that separates the
Presbytery from the concourse of people during Sacred Functions. 4: The principal wall of the
Chapel, in which may be admired the painting of the Last Judgment by the hand of Michel
Angelo Buonarroti. 5: The great Vault / of the Chapel, painted by the same Michel Angelo,
portraying the Creation of the World, with a compendium of the Story of the Old Testament.
6: Spaces between the lunettes above the windows, portraying Prophets and Sibyls, also painted
by Michel Angelo. 7, 8, 9, 10: Portraits of various Holy Popes painted / on the piers interposed
between the windows. 11, 12, 13, 14, 15, 16: Six of the paintings running around the interior of the
Attic of the Chapel, among which the one numbered 11 depicts Moses with Zipporah, when she
circumcised her son, a work by Luca Signorelli da Cortona; the one numbered 12 depicts / Moses
taking revenge on the Egyptian who murdered one of the Israelites, painted by Alessandro Filippi
Fiorentino; the one numbered 13 depicts the drowning of Pharaoh in the Red Sea, a work by
Cosimo Rosselli Fiorentino; the one numbered 14 portrays the adoration of the Golden Calf /
painted by the same artist; the one numbered 15 portrays the fire that rained down upon Corah,
Datan and Abiron, a work by Alessandro Botticelli; the one numbered 16, shows Moses, who,
before dying, reads the Holy Testament to the Hebrews, a work by Luca Signorelli da Cortona.
17: Six more paintings / also representing a few of the principal events of the New Testament,
works of other celebrated painters of that century, among them the famous Pietro Perugino,
director and master of many other artists for the same paintings / In Rome, by the Calcografia
(engraving office) of the Reverend Apostolic Chamber in the Curia Innocenziana, 1766.*

In 1766 the Calcografia Camerale, the papal engraving office in Rome, published this large
print depicting the interior of the Sistine Chapel looking toward the presbytery, with the ancient
papal throne visible beyond the choir screen. Executed by Francesco Barbazza according to a
design by Francesco Panini, son of the painter Gian Paolo (1691–1765), one of the most famous
scene painters (*vedutisti*) of Rome in his time, the etching includes a long caption that sup-
plies information about the stages of the construction and decoration of the chapel. Numbers
inserted in the image are linked to detailed explanations in the legend. The artist gave his
attention not only to the work of Michelangelo but also to the fifteenth-century frescoes on the
walls—a sign, perhaps, of the emerging fortune of the "primitives." In fact, the rather fanci-
ful reproductions of all the paintings share a common technique, thus wiping out all stylistic
diversity. Of the small figures that populate the scene, only a handful represent the faithful in
prayer; the foreground to the left is conspicuously occupied by a group of visitors glancing
upward in admiration, or perhaps to follow the explanations of a *cicerone*—a tourist guide.
The preparatory drawing for the work, signed and dated by Panini in 1766, is preserved in the
Kupferstichkabinett in Berlin.

   This beautiful print is not listed in the catalogue of images depicting the Sistine Chapel
that was compiled by Alida Moltedo in 1991.

P.R.

BIBLIOGRAPHY

Ferdinando Arisi, *Gian Paolo
Panini* (Milan, 1961), 287–88;
Charles de Tolnay, *L'omaggio
a Michelangelo di Albrecht
Dürer* (Rome, 1972), 14;
Ferdinando Arisi, *Gian Paolo
Panini e i fasti della Roma del
'700* (Rome, 1986), 200, 210;
Alida Moltedo, *La Sistina
riprodotta*, exh. cat. (Rome,
1991).

Della Cappella Sistina nel Palazzo Apostolico Vaticano, edificata dal Pontefice Sisto IV per opera di Baccio Pintelli, Architetto Fiorentino, e adornata sotto i Pontefici Giulio II Clemente VII e Paolo III.

1 Estremità sacra delle Altare della Cappella. 2 Soglio Pontificio, su la cui dritta proseguono gli stalli del Sacro Collegio. 3 Cancelli che dividono il Presbiterio dal concorso del popolo nelle Sacre Funzioni. 4 Parete principale della Cappella, in cui mirasi dipinto il Giudizio universale di mano di Michel Angelo Buonarroti. 5 La gran volta della Cappella, dipinta dal medesimo Michel Angelo, e rappresentante la Creazione del Mondo, con un compendio della storia del Testamento vecchio. 6 Spazj fra le lunette di sopra le finestre, rappresentanti Profeti e Sibille, dipinti anch'essi da Michel Angelo. 7, 8, 9, 10 Effigie di diversi Santi Pontefici dipinti ne' pilastri frapposti alle finestre. 11, 12, 13, 14, 15, 16 Sei quadri di quei che girano intorno all'Aula della Cappella, e fra quali il segnato con 11 rappresenta Mosè con Sefora, allor che questa circoncide il figliuolo; opera di Luca Signorelli da Cortona; il segnato col 12 rappresenta Mosè che si vendica dell'Egizio uccisore d'uno degl'Israeliti; dipinto da Alessandro Filippi Fiorentino; il segnato col 13 rappresenta la sommersione di Faraone nel Mar Rosso; lavoro di Cosimo Rosselli Fiorentino; il segnato col 14 figura l'adorazione del Vitello d'oro dipinto dal medesimo; il segnato col 15 figura il fuoco piovuto sopra Core, Datan ed Abiron; opera di Alessandro Botticelli; e il segnato col 16 mostra Mosè, che, prima di morire, legge il Sacro Testamento agli Ebrei; opera di Luca Signorelli da Cortona. 17 Altri sei quadri rappresentanti anch'essi alcuni fatti principali del Testamento nuovo, opere di altri celebri dipintori di quel Secolo, e fra gli altri del famoso Pietro Perugino, direttore e maestro di molti altri autori de'medesimi quadri.

In Roma dalla Calcografia della Rev. Camera Apostolica presso la Curia Innocenziana l'anno 1766.

Selected Bibliography

Ames-Lewis, Francis, and Paul Joannides, eds. *Reactions to the Master: Michelangelo's Effect on Art and Artists in the Sixteenth Century*. Burlington, Vt., 2003.

Barocchi, Paola. *Michelangelo e la sua scuola. I disegni di Casa Buonarroti e degli Uffizi*. Florence, 1962–64.

Bull, George, comp. and trans. *Michelangelo: Life, Letters, and Poetry*. New York, 1999.

Chapman, Hugo. *Michelangelo Drawings: Closer to the Master*. New Haven, 2005.

Condivi, Asconio. *Vita di Michelagnolo Buonarroti* (1553). Edited by E. Spina Barelli. Milan, 1964; Eng. trans., Oxford, 1976.

Connor, James A. *The Last Judgment: Michelangelo and the Death of the Renaissance*. New York, 2009.

Dotson, Esther G. "An Augustinian Interpretation of Michelangelo's Sistine Ceiling." Pts. 1 and 2. *Art Bulletin* 61, no. 2 (June 1979): 223–56; 61, no. 3 (Sept. 1979): 405–29.

Ettlinger, L. D. *The Sistine Chapel before Michelangelo: Religious Imagery and Papal Primacy*. Oxford, 1965.

Franklin, David. *Leonardo da Vinci, Michelangelo, and the Renaissance in Florence*. Exh. cat. Ottawa and New Haven, 2005.

Goffen, Rona. *Renaissance Rivals: Michelangelo, Leonardo, Raphael, Titian*. New Haven, 2004.

Graham-Dixon, Andrew. *Michelangelo and the Sistine Chapel*. London, 2008.

Hall, James. *Michelangelo and the Reinvention of the Human Body*. London, 2005.

Hibbard, Howard. *Michelangelo*. Cambridge, Mass., 1985.

Hirst, Michael. *Michelangelo and His Drawings*. New Haven, 1988.

———, and Jill Dunkerton. *Making and Meaning: The Young Michelangelo*. London, 1994.

King, Ross. *Michelangelo and the Pope's Ceiling*. New York, 2003.

Lisner, Magrit. *Il crocifisso di Michelangelo in Santo Spirito*. Munich, 1964.

Luchinat, Cristina Acidini. *The Medici, Michelangelo, and the Art of Late Renaissance Florence*. Exh. cat. New Haven and Detroit, 2002.

Nagel, Alexander. *Michelangelo and the Reform of Art*. New York, 2000.

Pietrangeli, Carlo, et al. *The Sistine Chapel: The Art, the History, and the Restoration*. New York, 1986.

Procacci, Ugo. *La Casa Buonarroti a Firenze*. Milan, 1965.

Ragionieri, Pina. *Michelangelo: Drawings and Other Treasures from the Casa Buonarroti, Florence*. Exh. cat. Atlanta, 2001.

———. *Michelangelo: The Man and the Myth*. Exh. cat. Syracuse, NY, 2008.

Steinberg, Leo. "Michelangelo's 'Last Judgment' as Merciful Heresy." *Art in America* 63 (1975): 49–63.

Vasari, Giorgio. *La vita di Michelangelo nelle redazioni del 1550 e del 1568*. Edited and with commentary by Paola Barocchi. Milan and Naples, 1962.

———. *Le vite de' più eccellenti pittori, scultore, e architettori*. Edited by Paola Barocchi and Rosanna Bettarini. Florence, 1967–87.

Wallace, William E. *Michelangelo: The Artist, the Man and His Times*. New York, 2009.

———. *Michelangelo: The Complete Sculpture, Painting, Architecture*. Westport, Conn., 1998.

———. "Michelangelo's Assistants in the Sistine Chapel." *Gazette des Beaux-Arts* (December 1987): 203–16.

Wilde, Johannes. *Italian Drawings in the Department of Prints and Drawings in the British Museum: Michelangelo and His Studio*. London, 1953.

Wisch, Barbara. "Vested Interest: Redressing Jews on Michelangelo's Sistine Ceiling." *Artibus et historiae* 48 (2003): 143–72.